PRAISE FOR *SI*

"Story rules when you want to influence others and this book is a must read if you want to rule the world of storytelling. Full of punchy narratives and science, Six Second Stories will show you how to do the most in the least amount of time."

> — **DR. PAUL J. ZAK,** Director of Center for Neuroeconomics Studies at Claremont Graduate University, Author of *Trust Factor: The Science of Creating High Performance Companies*

"In a world that continues to democratize the medium of storytelling — from the speakers on stages at TEDx events to the iPhone journalists helping to spur long overdue cultural revolution — it is critical that you know how to tell your story through the lens and onto the screen. Lucky for you (and me), Rain has created a resource to help us do exactly that without stress and overwhelm through what's become my new go-to guide for video storytelling."

> — **MIKE GANINO,** Creator of the Mike Drop Method for Public Speaking and Storytelling Former Executive Producer TEDx Cambridge

"Storytelling is one of the most powerful tools in any marketer's tool belt, and in this book, Rain teaches how to master both the art and science of story."

> — **MELANIE DEZIEL,** Author of *The Content Fuel Framework*

"Rain is a leader who truly cares about the work he shares with the world, that's why I know this book will impact so many who read it. There's so much truth behind his words on why telling your story is so important and needed. If you've been on the fence with sharing your story with the world, this is the book you need to be reading."

> — **ALEXA CARLIN,** Author of *Adaptable*

"If you want to stop feeling like you are drowning in a sea of sameness, then Six Second Stories is your life preserver. Rain Bennett takes you on his riveting personal journey and gives you the tools to learn to tell your own stories that inspire action."

> — **JOHN LIVESAY,** Keynote Speaker on Sales & Storytelling, Author of *Better Selling Through Storytelling*, TEDx Speaker

"Rain layers the information in such a way that by the end of the book, you not only know the history of storytelling, the science behind it, the psychology behind it, the impact because of it, but you also learn how to do it in the traditional sense and more modern-day digital sense. You may not become a master storyteller overnight, but you will have all the necessary components, tools, strategies, and prompts to help you activate the great storyteller that is in all of us after reading this book."

> — **TROY SANDIDGE,** Global B2B Marketing Strategist

"Because running experiments is the true secret to becoming a better storyteller, Rain narrates his own learning journey so well, by the time you finish this book you will feel like you have enough "experience" to run your own experiments."

> — **ANNETTE SIMMONS,** Author of The Story Factor and Whoever Tells the Best Story Wins

"Rain deftly uses his own stories and those of his clients to SHOW readers, vulnerably and powerfully, how to craft compelling stories that connect. A storyteller's storyteller, he takes his reader—and it reads like he is speaking to YOU!—through every part of story crafting so they, too, can master structure, know what stories to tell, and understand how to do it briefly and brilliantly in video and beyond. This is a terrific book with so much value for ANY reader–whether you're experienced or just beginning your story journey. And I promise you'll identify with a few of his heartfelt and real personal stories."

> — **KATHY KLOTZ-GUEST,** MA, MBA, Keynote Speaker, Improv Comedian, and Author of *Stop Boring Me!*

SIX SECOND STORIES

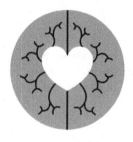

Maximize Your Impact in Minimal Time with VIDEO Storytelling

B. RAIN BENNETT

FLYING FLOUNDER PUBLISHING
CHAPEL HILL, NC

SIX SECOND STORIES:
Maximize Your Impact in Minimal Time with Video Storytelling

Published in the United States of America by

flying
flounder
PUBLISHING

ISBN: 978-1-7362135-1-3 (paperback)
ISBN: 978-1-7362135-2-0 (ebook)

Edited by: Chandler Comes
Cover Design: Rock & Roar Creative
Illustrations: Rock & Roar Creative
Interior Design and Typesetting: Rock & Roar Creative

See more work from B. Rain Bennett at
www.rainbennett.com

DEDICATION

to my children, Bellamy and Bishop:

Above all else, I hope I impart onto you the importance of persistence. Even when, like my journey writing this book, something takes you three times longer than what you expected, if you truly want it, you must keep going.

Also, it is you, with all your sleepless nights and interrupted mornings, that caused this book to take so long to write. And it wouldn't have been as good otherwise, so thank you.

CONTENTS

INTRODUCTION

What I'm about to share in this book started with a revelation I had when I was working as an independent filmmaker on my first feature-length documentary, *Raise Up: The World is Our Gym*. The film won "Best of the Fest" at the Hip Hop Film Festival in New York City, received global distribution through Red Bull TV, and changed how I would create my work for the rest of my life. I'm here to talk about that last part.

Let me explain.

In 2014, I stood with my DSLR camera as one of 30 camera operators at the famous Luzhniki Stadium in Moscow shooting what was known as the Street Workout World Championship. "Street Workout" was a name that post-Soviet countries gave to the freestyle calisthenics culture that had spread across the globe in the previous ten years, due in large part to the rise of social media. This new fitness-culture-turned-sport was growing fast and it was incredible to watch. When I paused to look around and marvel at the scene that day at the World Championship, I noticed that 29 of those 30 cameras were pointed at the athlete on stage, but mine was pointed in the other direction - one lone wolf camera going against the pack. I was capturing the other athletes nervously warming up, the audience rising to their feet during a big move, and the staff of the federation frantically trying to find the musical act for intermission.

Here's the difference I realized: while other camera operators captured flashy footage for recap videos and highlight reels on YouTube, I was telling a story.

Once I made the observation that I was doing something different, it was like I couldn't "un-see" it. I had suddenly discovered the value proposition for my business, my big "why," and the core of storytelling.

Well, it wasn't exactly a discovery. Like I said, it was more of a revelation. All of the dots had been there, but this was the moment I saw all the connections. You've probably also had moments like these in your life where several ideas have been percolating just under the surface, only to suddenly come together in a way that makes sense of what feels like EVERYTHING.

This was that moment for me in Moscow in 2014.

In that moment, I also realized how to articulate what I wanted to disrupt about the culture of calisthenics and independent film-making as a whole. Hell, I hadn't even realized I wanted to disrupt the culture until that moment. Here's how I had previously felt: I didn't have a great camera and I wasn't even that comfortable using it. I barely had any equipment and what I did have was cheap and borrowed from friends. I had no team, no resources to use, and no money. I felt overworked and overstressed all while trying to be super creative and sometimes it was so daunting that I even struggled to make it to shoots. I wasn't that technically skilled as a filmmaker. So I struggled to get the exposure right, or manually focus the lens, and definitely didn't know how to get that professional "blurred background" look in my interviews. That also meant that my editing style was super basic. I was terrible at things like motion graphics -- a growing field and aspect of video storytelling -- that could make my footage more visually captivating. To sum it up simply, I felt inadequate. Incapable. I felt like an impostor.

But I knew what made a good story. I knew what made a good cut -- what felt right when two video clips came together. I knew what was compelling and emotional for people. I knew how to empathize with my interview subjects and get the best, most in-depth and poignant responses from them. I didn't know all the technical stuff, but I did know the heart of a good story. I didn't know the science, but I knew the art.

And I realized that if I did *those* things well, I wouldn't need to rely on technical tools.

So my mindset shifted from "I can't make my video as good as the YouTube videos," to "I don't *want* to make those kinds of videos!" (And I truthfully didn't.) The problem I had with them was, no matter how cool these videos were, most of them looked the same and outside of an initial response of how cool they looked, they didn't capture the depth of the culture. They didn't show what truly made this new sport a worldwide movement. "Calisthenics" is a word of Greek origin (*kalos sthenos*) that loosely translates "beauty + strength."

The YouTube videos captured the strength. But I wanted to capture the beauty.

I traveled to over 15 countries in those two years making *Raise Up*.

During that time, I noticed a major shift in the content culture across the globe where video creators were no longer just "professional" filmmakers or video production company owners like me, but they were now hobbyists, too. It was everyone! And they had just as much access, and just as much know-how, as the professionals. Cameras were smaller, more user-friendly, and most importantly, cheaper. The barrier to entry in the video production game was gone. There were no more gatekeepers. And because of that, there was a huge new population of these content creators.

Now, over five years later, almost all of us are content creators. When I look around at the myriad of social media platforms, great content creators aren't just filmmakers, musicians, writers, TV show hosts, radio disc jockeys, dancers or artists like in the years of past. In the United States alone, there are about 295 million social media users. That's over 75% of the population! By 2025, that number is expected to rise to about 320 million people.[1] Even if you say you "hate social media," I'd be willing to bet you have an account or two you still use. But if you have a business, you almost certainly have some presence on social media -- or at least, you should. Even if that business Instagram profile only has 137 followers, someone told you to create an account and you did.

That's because there has never been a more direct, more effective, or cheaper way to send your messages to your customers and grow your client base or community than social media. It's no longer just big brands with huge advertising budgets. Now it's small business owners, entrepreneurs, nonprofit communication directors, and influencers growing their personal brands—basically anyone in charge of their team's (or their own) marketing.

The playing field has leveled. Sure, the big brands can still put more advertising dollars behind social media ads and boosted posts than you can, but you don't *need* to do that anymore. You have a direct line to your customers, clients, and communities. And if you know how to communicate with them clearly and effectively, you can grow your community, strengthen your client relationships, increase your sales and donations, and most importantly, deepen the impact you have on the lives of the people you serve.

But there's a new problem.

Like me not having the backing of Netflix or another big streaming channel for my film, you probably don't have the budget or teams that Nike, Apple, and Budweiser have to tell great stories that move your audience. And my guess would be that you also might not be a professional filmmaker, writer, or artist that then found yourself in this business role. You're probably overworked and perhaps underpaid—but almost definitely under-resourced.

You have a super small team (or no team, like me), barely any money to spend, and you feel like a one-person-band trying to manage the melody and rhythm of 13 different instruments. Each day it seems like there is a new tool that the marketing world tells you that you need to buy, a new app that's supposed to make your work easier and faster, or a new social media platform that everyone says you must be on now. This can cause multiple issues. You can either be so overwhelmed by all the options and not knowing which ones are best suited for you that it creates "analysis paralysis" and you do nothing. You keep putting it off and the marketing world keeps passing you by. Or you experience "FOMO" (fear of missing out) and it causes you to bounce from new gidget to new gadget too quickly ("shiny object syndrome") or abandon the strategy you've created too quickly ("ship jumping syndrome") in an attempt to keep up with the Joneses, but without ever give your current strategy a chance or asking yourself if the new strategy (or app/camera/social media platform) makes sense for your business. Have I used enough trendy expressions yet??

The main point is, like me in 2014, you need help.

You need a mindset shift. Stop looking for (or waiting for) some magical tool that is going to come along and quickly make you do your job better, but is somehow super easy to learn how to use. Remember, no tool is better than the hand that holds it.

Instead, you need to leverage the timeless skill of storytelling. Then, as you continue down your content creation path, you will eventually get better, and you will accumulate more tools to add to your toolbox. Those tools will definitely make your job easier in many ways. But for now, you just need to start. And when you don't have a lot of tools or money, the best way to make an impact is to communicate directly to your audience in the way that humans have communicated with each other for millennia: stories.

————————————

Why I fell in love with calisthenics culture was, yes, first because it was so visually stimulating and appealing, but the only reason I decided to dedicate five years of my life (and a lot more of my money) was that I saw that there was something deeper there. I saw that there was a story. That story was about the culture of this emerging sport known as freestyle calisthenics (depending on where you were geographically) and how it was changing the lives of young men and women around the world.

The Street Workout World Championship that summer in Moscow was one of the last days of filming I did for *Raise Up*. I'd been shooting interviews, training sessions, and competitions since the spring of 2012. At that point, I was living in New York and had been following the growing calisthenics culture that had been taking over the city since the early 2000s. There were several "teams," (or loose organizations, really) that had formed all over the city and almost all of them had some form of the word "bar" in their names in reference to the pullup bar -- the mainstay of their exercise regimens. It started with a group called the Bartendaz around 2003, which was an offshoot of a community youth empowerment organization created by Hassan "Giant" Yasin called G.I.A.N.T. Thinking. Soon after, there were teams popping up all over the five boroughs with names like Bar-barians, Barstarzz, Barmasters Xtreme, and Beastmode. Not all of them were community organizations like the Bartendaz, but every one of them impacted their communities in profound ways.

That's what made me follow this culture for my documentary. The moves that these men and women were doing with their bodies were incredible -- flipping and twisting over the bars in unimaginable ways. But it was how they shape the culture of their neighborhoods that was story worthy. One these practitioners of calisthenics mastered the basic moves and then advanced moves, they started putting those moves together in creative ways. Birthed out of the same parks where hip hop started, it was part of the same culture that brought the world breakdancing, graffiti art, and rapping. And like those subcultures, freestyle calisthenics became an art form. People developed their own styles. Some were dynamic and explosive others were smooth and rhythmic in their movements. It became a way for people to express themselves. And when it did, it attracted the youth -- always searching

7

for new ways to find their voice. As a result, they flocked to the parks and this style of exercise became a community movement. It was getting kids off the streets, out of gangs, and off of drugs. It was helping them find confidence and social skills. They stayed out of trouble. They got better grades. They started caring about the food they put in their body!

But it wasn't just the children who benefited from this movement. Calisthenics is made up of bodyweight exercises, it could be done anywhere with no equipment required. And *that* meant it could be done for free. And that meant that the barrier to entry (like an expensive gym membership) to getting fit was eliminated. But it also meant that the "bar" was available to anyone. It democratized fitness. That brought people together from different social groups that wouldn't normally congregate together. The elderly came to train as well as the youth. Black people, white people. Cop and ex-convicts. Men, women. Rich, poor. This style of training was not only strengthening individuals, it was strengthening communities.

Once I realized the social component of the calisthenics culture and saw that there was real heart to it, I knew I had to tell this story. From there, the project evolved from just a neat idea for a video about a New York City-based fitness community to a full-length feature film about a global movement.

All the other cameras that day in Moscow were focused on the main action happening -- the athlete onstage. And there were good reasons to focus on that type of footage. A big part of the lifestyle was the use of social media like YouTube and Instagram. People would post their workouts or new moves that they'd learned on their social media channels and watch their videos quickly go viral. During the competitions, fans of this new sport around the world would be so interested in who was winning and what new moves had been done that there was a race to see who could put out the first YouTube video. I remember sitting on the bus leaving that night and my friend Dennis was already cutting a video on his laptop. That video got over four million views.

There was a big difference in what content creators like Dennis were doing and what I was doing. In reality, most of them probably didn't know what I was doing. I had been the weird American traveling around the world filming all these different people working out and not posting any of my video clips. The status quo was to make an awesome three-to-seven minute highlight reel with funky graphics and some dubstep music behind it to help the moves look cooler than they actually were. Don't get me wrong, many of the things these guys and girls were doing with their bodies were amazing. But when the editors used "slo-mo" or paused the motion or added a flash of motion graphics, it would make it look way cooler.

I'm not trying to throw shade on the video quality of those highlight reels. The reels these camera operators created during this time were awesome and helped propel the culture to the global level. But even though the YouTube videos were effective at growing the culture, they just didn't have the depth that I wanted to have. It seemed like so many of the video creators were focused on the video effects they could lay on top of their footage, the loud music which they edited in sync with the rhythm of the moves, and flashy transitions from scene to scene.. But they never asked themselves what, if anything, all these devices really added to the story. To me, that approach is like focusing on the curtains on the windows of a house you're building when you haven't even gotten the frame of the house built. The story is the framework of any video. That doesn't mean you don't pay attention to the fine details (like the curtains of the house or the motion graphics in the video) and use them to enhance your project. You just don't do that out of order. If you have a solid structure and a simple story, you can still create something that resonates with people. But if you don't have the structure and instead you just have a loose grouping of visuals, effects, and sounds, then you will never create something that sinks its hooks in the hearts of your audience and has the lasting impact you seek to have.

That lasting impact you seek really comes from effecting change in your audience -- inspiring them to take action. Perhaps the biggest lesson I learned along my journey is that stories have the ability to create that change. If someone watching a calisthenics highlight reel on YouTube was already into calisthenics, they'd watch every minute of it. Like preaching to a choir, they're already sold. If someone was already into fitness, they'd also be interested in watching the video. They may even start practicing calisthenics in their own lives afterwards seeing it. However, if someone wasn't in shape, but they wanted to be, the videos did nothing to convert them. All the videos did was make those people feel like they'd never be able to do the amazing things the calisthenics athletes could do with their bodies, and they'd certainly never have their physiques. That's because those videos were highlight reels. They only showed the highlights! But people don't connect with sheer awesomeness. They aren't inspired to make changes in their lives by seeing someone's highlights. People are inspired by struggle. They're inspired by watching someone overcome obstacles. They're inspired by stories. And if a story is told well, it will drive them to take action.

When I realized this, I intentionally stopped the way I had been shooting my documentary and doubled down on the simple storytelling strategy. I stopped recording every interview possible just because people were there and I thought I should include them. I actually shot LESS of the competitions and moves, now that I knew I was documenting the culture and not the competitions. This wasn't even videography. This was a film. I focused more on the narrative and how all the different footage I had accumulated actually tied together into a single story. If someone, even someone I liked, didn't help move the story forward, I had to cut their portion from the movie. It was hard. There's an old adage often attributed to William Faulkner (and several others) that says "in writing, you must kill all your darlings," meaning to be okay eliminating any words, subplots, or even characters we love that do nothing to make the story better. It's very hard for many storytellers to do. It was even harder when those "darlings" had actually become your friends in real life.

After the World Championship in 2014, my work really started. It took two and a half years before we finally released *Raise Up* on Redbull TV. During that time, I continued using my strategy of keeping it simple, focusing on the story, and using what I had access to. The tool that I had access to that provided the most help was undoubtedly my audience. I involved them in the process. I let them into my world and brought them along my journey making the documentary. I held test screenings, private screenings, public screenings, and even focus groups to get their feedback. I listened to them. Every screening I held, I also hosted a panel discussion about the themes of the film (health, self-empowerment, and community building). I created conversations with them. As the months turned to years and my film got better, my team of supporters grew. My crew grew, too. I was able to secure multiple investors to help get us to the finish line. We screened it all across the country and even in Norway, the Netherlands, and Equatorial Guinea on the west coast of Africa. We won "Best of the Fest" at the Hip Hop Film Festival in Harlem, where I shot the very first footage for the film in 2012. And then five years later in October 2017, Red Bull put out a video on their official Facebook page promoting the film's premiere on its streaming channel Red Bull TV. It gained over three million views. And since then, my favorite messages to receive have been those including photos from people on planes who find the movie among the in-flight entertainment choices.

But none of that would have happened if I didn't follow my heart... and just start.

Personally, I like Stephen King's take on the Faulkner "darlings" quote. In his nonfiction book *On Writing*, King wrote, "Kill your darlings, kill your darlings, even when it breaks your egocentric little scribbler's heart, kill your darlings."[2]

Now in this quote, King was referring to the overconfidence that one's ego can create. But don't forget, ego creates a lot of insecurity, as well. I'd be willing to bet that most of what is preventing you from starting is not actually your access to the right tools, money, or education on the topic. It's your head. It's that story that you're telling yourself -- that you're not ready, that it's not time, and that you're not qualified enough.

All of these thoughts in your head are actually ego-centric in nature. It's you thinking about you. If your focus is fully on your audience, you will just start creating your content and sharing your stories because you know you have something that can help them. When you hesitate, or procrastinate, or any-other-ate, it's because of your ego. You don't want to fail. You don't want to look stupid or make a mistake. But if you listen to your audience and not the story you're telling yourself inside your head, your audience will tell you what they need, and ultimately end up guiding you on your path to guide them.

Let me give you an example. If you were stranded on the side of a road with a flat tire and I saw you, knowing that I had a jack and a tire iron in my trunk but I just waved and drove past you, that would be pretty crappy of me, right? Well that's what you're doing to your audience when you aren't letting them know what you can offer to their lives or businesses. You have a responsibility to let people know that you can help them. And video is the most powerful way you can do that on the information superhighway known as the internet. With the reach the internet gives you, you won't have to tell one stranded customer at a time. Your customers, clients, and community will tell people themselves because of the shareability of stories. Good stories stick, but great stories spread.

So, if you want to create videos to tell the story of your personal brand or your business, but you don't know much about the gizmos and gadgets that filmmakers use to create visuals, effects, and sound, I've got good news for you:

You can make a huge impact just by sharpening your storytelling skills.

And if you want to impact the world through the stories you tell, I've got even better news for you. I'm going to show you how to maximize that impact in minimal time.

What we know is the tools will always change. The platforms will always change. You are doing yourself a disservice if you limit your abilities by attaching them too closely to the medium.

However, if you become expert storytellers, then whether you are using your smartphone, a microphone, a video camera, or just chatting at a networking event, you will be able to connect with people, communicate with them effectively, and, most importantly, inspire them to change.

The two things the calisthenics highlight reels did get right, besides the badass moves they featured, were the platforms (YouTube, Instagram, etc.) and the running time (usually 3-10 minutes). Most likely, this will be the kind of video storytelling you create for your business. You probably won't be producing feature-length documentaries. Although there can be a lot of benefit for telling long form brand stories, as well (we'll touch on that later). You're going to need to know how to tell a compelling story in the shortest amount of time possible. In just the past few years, we've seen the standard advertisement time go from 30 seconds down to 15, down to 10, and now even down to just six seconds. But with such a short amount of time, the challenge is creating a strong emotional connection with your audience when they haven't even had time to process what they've seen.

In 2018, I created a video marketing company to answer just that question: "Can you tell a great story in six seconds?"

Of course, you can tell what's considered a story in six seconds. But a great story is one that moves an audience emotionally. And a great brand story also inspires that audience to take action. And that is incredibly hard to do in such a short time.

But with the current demands of social media and the need to capture your audience's attention quickly before they pivot to any one of the myriad of other options they have, you have to maximize your impact in minimal time.

And the most effective way to do that is through video storytelling.

In this book, I'll give you a system you can use to start telling stories that will resonate with your audience. These are the keys to the storytelling kingdom.

In Part One, I get into the sausage with you to discover how storytelling works. I'll talk about why human beings love stories so much, what stories do to our brains, and the critical components that all great stories have in common.

In Part Two, I get into the "how to" of storytelling so that you can follow a simple system to choose the right stories to tell your audience and the tools to use to execute them.

Finally, in Part Three, I will show you how to tell great stories even in a super short amount of time by amplifying your hook and your call to action, cutting out the unnecessary pieces, and getting straight to the heart of your story and the hearts of your audience.

After reading this book, you will have the understanding you need to take action immediately. You will learn how to stand out in a sea of sameness. You will learn how to make your stories stick in the minds of your audience and spread to others who need your message. You will learn how to tell compelling stories at any time, with any tool. You will learn how to communicate your messages more clearly and that will help you establish deeper, more meaningful relationships with your clients, customers, and community. You will find a deeper passion in the world you do because you've uncovered the true meaning behind it. But most of all, you will be able to effect positive change in the lives of the people you serve.

To my mind, motivating change is the heart and soul of storytelling. And if your goal is to maximize impact, the first thing you need to know is how storytelling works.

PART ONE

HOW DOES STORYTELLING WORK?

Chapter 1
WHY ARE STORIES IMPORTANT?

Why do people love stories so much? And why do gurus and experts keep telling you that you need to use storytelling in your marketing strategy?

Well first of all, stories are, always have always been, and always will be uniquely human. It's not just an art form of expression, it's the way we communicate. From the early days of *homo sapiens*, we actually used stories for survival. In the beginning, we used them to build trust among other humans (spoiler alert: we still do!).

Suppose I bumped into another human in the backwoods of Beaufort County, North Carolina, where I was raised, thousands of years ago. I wouldn't have known if they were friend or foe. And I wouldn't have had too much time to figure it out before I was at risk of being bludgeoned with a blunt object. So we'd examine each other. We'd ask questions. We'd share stories.

Our interaction might go something like this: "Oh, what's that? You know my friend Brantley Barefoot? Wait, you actually grew up together in Pinetown (a little town 15 minutes from my home-town)? Well tell me this, who's your grandmama? Oh hell, man. We're COUSINS!"

Now, instead of trying to beat each other to death, we'd be head-ed down to the banks of the Pamlico River together to go flounder gigging. Alternatively, if he were related to my rival Michael Knox, that interaction would have ended a lot differently.

In Yuval Noah Harari's nonfiction historical epic *Sapiens*, he de-scribes how storytelling led homo sapiens to become the leaders of the world.

> "*Sapiens rule the world, because we are the only animal that can cooperate flexibly in large numbers. We can create mass cooperation networks, in which thousands and millions of complete strangers work together towards common goals. One-on-one, even ten-on-ten, we humans are embarrass-ingly similar to chimpanzees. Any attempt to understand our unique role in the world by studying our brains, our bodies, or our family relations, is doomed to failure. The real difference between us and chimpanzees is the mysterious glue that en-ables millions of humans to cooperate effectively.*
>
> *This mysterious glue is made of stories, not genes. We coop-erate effectively with strangers because we believe in things like gods, nations, money and human rights. Yet none of these things exists outside the stories that people invent and tell one another. There are no gods in the universe, no nations, no money and no human rights—except in the common imagina-tion of human beings. You can never convince a chimpanzee to give you a banana by promising him that after he dies, he will get limitless bananas in chimpanzee Heaven. Only Sa-piens can believe such stories. This is why we rule the world, and chimpanzees are locked up in zoos and research labora-tories.*[3]

After using stories to build trust with one another, we used them to create a feeling of belonging. You know… that feeling that we are all on a perpetual quest to find through our social groups, our religions, and even within groups of people who root for the same sports team? That feeling makes us feel good. It makes us feel safe. We *need* it. The need to belong to a group, on a primal level, also originated from our survival instincts. If our ancestors living in tribes were cast out of the group, left to fend for themselves, their chances of living a long and happy life would have plummeted dramatically. In other words, we needed to belong to a group.

What's interesting is that we still treat belonging to a group the same way, even though it is no longer a life-or-death situation. Psychologically, it still feels like it is. That's why we feel so much shame if we do something embarrassing or make public mistakes. Our primal fear, the "squirrel brain" as Seth Godin calls it—which is technically the amygdala and hasn't evolved much in the many millennia since the Cognitive Revolution—still makes us feel like we run the risk of being kicked out of our community and have to face predators and the harshness of Mother Nature alone. So when we can share common stories with one another, it gives us that sense of being part of a bigger group, and thus the feeling of being protected and safe. Sometimes, however, when people recognize that they belong to the same group as another person, it can create a bond that actually does influence life and death.

One of my favorite stories about stories goes way back in history to around 413 BCE during the Peloponnesian War. The Peloponnesian war was primarily between two Greek city-states, Athens and Sparta, and the oft-interchangeable supporting casts of cities that made up their respective "leagues"--the Delian League and the Peloponnesian League. The war lasted from 431 until 404 BCE. In 413, many of the Athenian soldiers were captured in Sicily and imprisoned in the city of Syracuse. They were left there for months, fed nothing but a pint of barley meal and a half-pint of water a day, as they waited to be sold as slaves. Clearly the Sicilians didn't really care if they died from hunger during the wait.

One of the most famous playwrights in history, Euripides, was from Athens during this era.

All Greeks were proud to call him their own, but Sicilians especially loved his work. So much so, that it saved the lives of Athenian prisoners that could recite his work. The guards would ask the prisoners if they knew some of his plays and the Athenians naturally would. It was their hometown boy! So they'd act out the plays and get extra food and water. And sometimes, if the prisoners would teach the guards as much of the plays as they knew, the guards would actually set them free!

> "For the Sicilians, it would seem, more than any other Hellenes outside the home land, had a yearning fondness for his poetry. They were forever learning by heart the little specimens and morsels of it which visitors brought them from time to time, and imparting them to one another with fond delight. In the present case, at any rate, they say that many Athenians who reached home in safety greeted Euripides with affectionate hearts, and recounted to him, some that they had been set free from slavery for rehearsing what they remembered of his works, and some that when they were roaming about after the final battle they had received food and drink for singing some of his choral hymns" (Plutarch, Life of Nicias, XXIX.2-3).[4]

This blows my mind. Storytelling can actually save lives! It's hard to find something analogous in my own life. But here's the best I can come up with. Dominique Wilkins, the NBA Hall of Famer also known as "The Human Highlight Reel," is from my hometown of "Little" Washington, North Carolina. Perhaps this would be like me telling the legendary stories of his time in high school and infamous dunks he made at 16 years old. I just can't imagine the police letting me out of jail after telling them how the Washington High School boys' basketball team still has the longest running win streak (3 seasons!) in the history of the state of North Carolina. I think it's cool, and maybe they would. But I'd still be behind bars—unless, of course, one of those guards happened to also be from Little Washington. We might feel like family then. We might feel like we belong to the same group and he *may* even feel inclined to hook me up with an extra phone call or at least refer me to a good lawyer.

This is the strength of storytelling. It's been a part of history and the fabric of our culture and society for millennia. It created bonds and connections between people. After an initial bond was created with people, it helped them feel like they belonged to a certain group. Then, they could trust one another. Once they had that trust built and knew they could be friendly and not try to kill one another, it opened up the opportunity for trade. That's because trust accelerates empathy. Once we trust each other, I can tell you what I need and 1) you'll believe me, and 2) you'll actually care enough to help. Then, you can see what you might have that could help me.

Harari explains further in *Sapiens*:

> At the heart of our mass cooperation networks, you will always find fictional stories that exist only in people's collective imagination. Two Catholics who have never met can nevertheless go together on crusade or pool funds to build a hospital because they both believe that God was incarnated in human flesh and allowed himself to be crucified to redeem our sins. Two Serbs who have never met might risk their lives to save one-another because both believe in the existence of the Serbian nation, the Serbian homeland, and the Serbian flag. Two lawyers who have never met can nevertheless combine efforts to defend a complete stranger because they all believe in the existence of laws, justice, human rights—and the money paid out in fees.
>
> Yet none of these things exists outside the stories that people invent and tell one another. There are no gods, no nations, no money and no human rights, except in our collective imagination. The truly unique trait of Sapiens is our ability to cre-

ate and believe fiction. All other animals use their communication system to describe reality. We use our communication system to create new realities. Of course not all fictions are shared by all humans, but at least one has become universal in our world, and this is money. Dollar bills have absolutely no value except in our collective imagination, but everybody believes in the dollar bill.[5]

The primal need to belong to a group isn't uniquely human. We see group behavior in hill-building ants, swarming bees, schools of fish, and several other animal species. But the ability to tell stories, create that bond and sense of belonging from them, and then cooperate and act on a massive, even global scale, is uniquely human. Thousands of years later, we're still relying on that and cooperation trust for our trade, and trade has become the backbone of our global society.

That's why commercials that resonate with us can evoke strong emotional reactions. That's why storytelling works so well in advertising. If you're reading this book, you've probably already heard this, or at least have heard that you need to incorporate storytelling in your marketing. It's kind of a marketing buzzword now and that's because people are finally understanding how powerful stories can be to market their ideas, products, or services. Any good marketer knows this, because storytelling is simply how humans communicate. Obviously it would work well when trying to sell one's products or services. But the industry got away from it for a while when advertising skyrocketed to popularity with the advent of television.

Seth Godin explains in his 2018 book, *This is Marketing*:

> For 100 years, marketing and advertising was the same thing. The CMO didn't decide on the product line or pricing or what the toxic waste policy should be. Instead, the measure of marketing has traditionally been, "How much money are you spending on advertising?"

Only in the last 20 years have we seen marketing change from spending money to interrupt people with advertising to market everything you make and everything you say. That involves making a promise to people about what they should expect when they do business with you.[6]

What we've seen in recent years is this shift back to storytelling to make those promises to our customers, clients, and communities. We live in the era of "fake news" and people feel like they're being lied to all the time. When they can tell something is an ad, they know they are just being sold to and don't trust the brand. What do you do when a commercial comes on the television? I hit the mute button on the remote control. What do you do when a pop-up appears on your computer screen? I frantically search for the "X" with my mouse to close out the window.

People crave transparency and authenticity and they don't like to feel pushed into buying something. That's what traditional advertising does. People want to have a reason to buy and they want to know what they're supporting with that purchase. They're yearning for connection, especially when it comes to where they choose to spend their money. That's what stories do. They don't push people into making a decision—they pull people into their storyworld and inspire them to take action.

In an interview, Godin was asked exactly how he defined "marketing," currently.

Well, the easy answer is, it's not advertising. And a lot of people have trouble right there because for 50 years it was advertising. Mad Men was all about this notion that if you ran enough ads – they didn't have to be good, you just had to run enough – they would pay for themselves. It was a perpetual motion machine of money. That ended a few years ago.

I like to describe marketing as "the art of telling a story that resonates with your audience and then spreads."[7]

Seth also famously said that "marketing is no longer about the stuff that you make, but about the stories you tell." The way we connect as humans is through shared experiences and emotions. And the way we communicate those experiences and emotions are through stories. That's all you're trying to do—make connections with your customers, clients, and communities. Once you establish those connections, it's up to you what you do with them. You can use them to convert sales, to encourage downloads and signups, to inspire donors, to accumulate members, and so much more. So if Seth and I, and every other marketer in between are screaming at you to tell stories in your marketing strategy, why aren't you doing it? Chances are, you think it's something reserved for expert artists or people with a natural talent to tell great stories. You probably think it's not something you could ever be great at, especially with everything else you have on your plate. Yeah, I used to think the same thing when I was making my movie.

Storytelling is, indeed, an art form that can resonate with people just like the Sistine Chapel or "Stairway to Heaven." When people hear a great story, it has the power to elicit an emotional response from them that connects them with the storyteller on a deep, heartfelt level. So much so, that one might think storytelling is some innate talent that only certain ordained individuals possess, clearly bestowed upon them by the divine touch of the gods.

A great storyteller can make you feel that way.

But what you might not understand is that storytelling, while indeed an art form, also has a science to its structure. Those amazing, compelling storytellers are actually following a formula.

And you can follow it, too.

Chapter 2
THE SCIENCE OF STORYTELLING

Leonardo da Vinci supposedly once said, "To develop a complete mind: study the science of art study the art of science. Learn how to see. Realize that everything connects to everything else." If anyone proved that art is based on science, Leonardo did. Stories are no different.

MY FIRST STORY COMPETITION

Every month or so, I perform in a "story slam" in North Carolina called The Monti. A "story slam" is a competitive storytelling event, much like a poetry slam, where a group of people (8, in this case) battle it out on stage by telling five minute stories based on a predetermined theme. Everyone who wants to tell a story puts their name in a hat and only eight are selected. There is a panel of judges who score based on criteria like: the structure of the story, the length of the story (over 5 minutes is a warning, over 6 minutes is a penalty), and of course, the impact the story has on the audience.

I had never competed in one of these events, but always wanted to. When I made it a goal to start public speaking more in 2018, I nervously signed up for a story slam with the theme "secrets." The night came and my very pregnant girlfriend and I arrived at a local music venue in Durham. There were hundreds of people there. I found the table where we could sign up and put my name in the hat, which was really just an empty beer pitcher. My heart was beating fast and I was doing breathing exercises in an attempt to slow it. After four storytellers went there was a brief intermission. I finished my beer and said, "Well, they probably won't call me, do you want to just go?" I was looking at the door, wondering if anyone would realize I snuck out even though I was supposed to tell a story. But no one knew I had signed up. What if they actually called my name and I wasn't there? Would that be worse? "No," my girlfriend replied, "this is what we came to do babe. You got this." We sat back down in our seats. They called my name next.

Thirty minutes later, I was onstage receiving my medal (there was no medal, they just called my name out, but in my mind there was a medal) after winning my first ever attempt at a story slam. I had also qualified to speak in the "Grand Slampionship" later that spring.

Here's the story I told:

> On Christmas Eves, and many other nights throughout
> the year, I slept in the bed with my big brother. He was
> seven years older than me, but we were super close. We'd
> stay up making up stories and giggling. He'd tell me that

he'd scratch my back if I scratched his and then act like he was asleep when it was his turn. Or he'd tickle me until I screamed and my mom would fling the door open and yell at us to get back to bed. Typical big brother stuff. And other times, he'd be really sweet. I remember him often humming "Greensleeves" until I fell asleep.

The spotlight on the stage was blinding and my heart was pounding. The silence of the audience was deafening, but a few little bits of laughter cut through and helped me relax.

Every Christmas Eve, we'd hear some bumping around the house - probably my parents putting together presents. And every year he'd tell me the same thing. He'd get real quiet and say, "Shhh....Rain listen! I think that's the reindeer on the roof." And I'd hunker down beside him and listen. "I hear it!" I'd say. And Beau would tell me that "We better go to bed, cause Santa will leave if we're still awake." And we'd hop back into bed, giggling our little asses off.

This particular night, we heard the thumping like the previous years. Same thing happened and we hopped back in bed to make sure Santa dropped off our presents. I laid down, closed my eyes and tried to go to sleep. Then BAM! We heard a thump, louder than we'd ever heard before, that shook the whole house. Beau hopped out of bed and ran to the door, me right behind him. We sprinted down the hall and turned the corner to the living room to see my dad holding my mom down by the hair and her swinging at him trying to break free.

I heard an audible gasp from the audience.

See, my dad was a drunk and the thumping we'd always heard wasn't the presents being put together. Apparently, he was worse around the holidays. But my brother had kept it from me.

We screamed at him to let her go but he wouldn't. "Get him off me, Beau!" my mom yelled.

Beau glanced down at the bottom of the Christmas tree and saw a brand new Wilson tennis racquet under the tree with a bow on it. He was supposed to find it a few hours later. He picked it up and walked towards my dad, 12 years old and terrified.

My dad's back was turned to him and Beau raised the racquet back and swung it like a baseball bat. Just as he swung, my dad turned towards him and the racquet came down on his eye, busting open his head. Blood went everywhere.

My dad screamed "You broke my goddamn head!" as he rushed to the sink. For some reason, even at 5, I remember thinking, "How can you break your head?" Even at 5 years old, I was an asshole about semantics.

Now the family was in "save drunk Daddy" mode and threw some paper towels in his head and all loaded in the station wagon. We were like a redneck version of the Griswalds, which I guess made us more like Uncle Eddie's family.

On the way there, Mom and Dad were debating on what to tell the doctors when they asked how'd it happen. They went back and forth for a while, my dad coming up with dumb excuses that made no sense, but finally they settled on that he was going outside to get some presents and fell off the steps onto the concrete under our carport.

We all went in, as a family, and watched as the ER nurses wheeled my dad down the hall. I heard him trying to explain what happened - giving them some ridiculous version of *what my mom had told him to say.*

I stood beside my mom holding her hand, her other arm was around Beau who was crying and hadn't said a word since we left.

I looked up and said, "Mama, why didn't we tell them what really happened?"

"Because baby, sometimes we don't tell people our family secrets."

When I ended on that line, the crowd erupted into applause. In my mind, they were giving a standing ovation, throwing roses on stage, and even one woman fainted and had to be carried out the back door. But even the reality of (just) an eruption of applause was still thrilling for me.

Clearly this was an emotional story. It may have created some emotions in you, whether you've experienced abuse or not. And I think for the audience, that was part of the reason why they reacted the way they did and a big part of the reason I won. The other seven storytellers told stories that were humorous in nature, seeking laughs. And while I had a few moments of comic relief designed to pop the tension, my story was anything but a comedy. It was tough to listen to. Hell, it was tough to tell in front of that many people. But being vulnerable and sharing my authentic story did two very important things: it allowed me to work through pain with a group of supportive people listening, and being vulnerable in front of them inspired the audience and made them feel a deeper connection with me. That's another hidden power of stories.

I knew it was a good story, in terms of structure. But I didn't know how it would resonate.

When I heard that gasp from the audience after I revealed

what was causing the thumping and bumping, I knew we were all connected. I *had* them. We were on this ride together and they could empathize with me. Once I had them, I knew I wasn't letting go until the story was over.

HOW STORIES ALTER YOUR BRAIN

There's an amazing thing that happens to people when they hear great stories. They experience what's known as "narrative transportation." The narrative transportation theory proposes that narrative transformation occurs when the audience experiences a feeling of entering the world of the story because of empathy for the characters and imagination of the plot. That means people hearing or watching a story feel like they are actually *in* the story!

So when I described the big thump that made Beau and I jump out of bed and how we sprinted down the hallway, the audience felt like they were, too. Their hearts were racing just like ours were. The tension grew. What was that loud noise? What were we going to see around the corner? At that moment, the audience and I were completely in sync. *That* is why the payoff was so huge when I revealed that my dad was holding my mom down by her hair. The audience didn't know what to expect behind that corner, just like my five-year-old self didn't. And that is why stories are so powerful to our brains.

Furthermore, when people see or hear a story, a process called "neural coupling" occurs, where neural pathways in the brains of the listeners light up and respond as if they are experiencing what's happening in the story themselves. That means the minds of the speaker and listeners look identical to each other. And that's the first connection that happens between humans with storytelling: a neurological one. I'd say that's a pretty damn powerful one.

NEURAL COUPLING

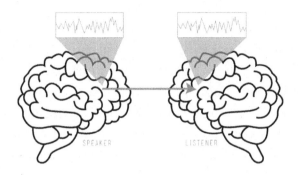

Years ago, a team of scientists at Princeton, led by Dr. Uri Hasson, had a woman tell a story while measuring her brain activity in a functional MRI (fMRI) scanner.[8] They then had a group of volunteers listen to the stories through headphones while they had their brains scanned. When the woman had activity in her insula, an emotional brain region, the listeners did too. When her frontal cortex lit up, so did theirs. By simply telling a story, the woman could effectively plant ideas, thoughts, and emotions into the listeners' brains. Hasson later looked at listening comprehension, as well. He found that the more the listeners understood the story, the more their brain activity mirrored the speaker's.

So when you listen to stories and understand them, your brain lights up in the same way and looks exactly like the person's brain who is telling the story. That means the storyteller and the story listener are completely linked on a brain level! This is huge for understanding communication and Hasson's study completely changed how we now view the power of stories. It's also a huge opportunity for you, no matter what you are trying to accomplish in your business. When you have the opportunity to tell a story, do not waste it. Think about how stories impact the brains of your customers and clients and use them to create a deeper understanding between what they are struggling with and what you have that can help them. If you're trying to convince someone of something, whether it's donating to your foundation or just entering your store, an essential part of it is getting them to understand you—to be on the same wavelength.

Both narrative transportation and neural coupling commonly happen when we watch movies. We cry when the main character gets her heart broken, even though we're not the ones standing there at the prom dance watching our boyfriend dance with another girl. We jump and scream when a ghost or goblin appears out of nowhere, just like the character on screen does. Good screenwriters know this fact, and that's how they can toy with us and our experience as an audience. Sometimes, they will even throw a false scare in there just to keep us on the edge of our seats.

Here's a real-life example from my childhood: I remember seeing my dad lying on the floor watching *Rocky IV* in the late 80s, screaming "hit him!" to the screen as Rocky and the evil Russian Ivan Drago duked it out in a battle that could potentially cause World War III. I sat right beside my dad, glued to the TV screen and doing my best impression of him. Both of our hearts were racing and we probably felt like we could take on the world. We felt like we were Rocky himself. In that moment, we were experiencing both narrative transportation and neural coupling. But what was also happening was that our dopamine levels were skyrocketing. The tension of the fight and agonizing victory, no matter how inevitable, had us screaming in delight. No drug could've done that. Well, my dad was pretty drunk, but still. You get the point.

Dopamine is one of several hormones that affect our moods and make storytelling effective. Technically, I believe they are considered neurotransmitters, but I am not a neuroscientist. And neither are you, probably, so let's keep it simple and call them hormones. Dr. Paul Zak, however, is a neuroscientist and he conducts groundbreaking research on how stories affect the brain. Zak is the founding director of the Center for Neuroeconomics Studies at Claremont Graduate University and is a pioneer in understanding the science of storytelling.

In an article for the *Harvard Business Review*, he writes:

> *It is quiet and dark. The theater is hushed. James Bond skirts along the edge of a building as his enemy takes aim. Here in the audience, heart rates increase and palms sweat. I know this to be true because instead of enjoying the movie myself, I am measuring the brain activity of a dozen viewers. For me, excitement has a different source: I am watching an amazing neural ballet in which a story line changes the activity of people's brains.*
>
> *Many business people have already discovered the power of storytelling in a practical sense – they have observed how compelling a well-constructed narrative can be. But recent scientific work is putting a much finer point on just how stories change our attitudes, beliefs, and behaviors.[9]*

THE STORYTELLING COCKTAIL

Dr. Zak is what I would consider to be the godfather of neuroeconomics, or the study of how and why the brain makes decisions. His work is fascinating to me, so I reached out and booked him on my podcast, *The Storytelling Lab* (there's a pun, here), and I got the chance to learn from him directly. One of his most popular studies looked at the impact of exactly what this book is about—video storytelling. Dr. Zak and his team used an animated cartoon story of a child with terminal brain cancer, named Ben, and his dad. Even just saying that little, I'm sure you already have some emotions emerging. Zak measured the blood of his research subjects before and after watching the video and analyzed what hormones the brain produced. There are three of these hormones that work together in what I call the Storytelling Cocktail. If you tell a great story, you will find that your audience's brain chemistry will in fact change, leaving them under the influence of your message.

The first one is dopamine. Dopamine is a pleasure hormone, and is usually produced when we feel some sort of reward—like following Rocky's heartbreaking journey in *Rocky IV*, losing his best friend and all his money, and then seeing him get revenge by beating the crap out of the evil Russian, Ivan Drago. Dopamine is elevated in the minds of your audience when a story is laid out in a certain structure. Like a rollercoaster ride, it should be full of rising tension and then the releasing of that tension, back and forth, ebbing and flowing so the audience can't wait to hear what happens next. Like "dope," they will crave it. And that will make your audience latch on to your story, be fully engaged, and stick around for the ultimate payoff (your call to action!).

The next hormone in the Storytelling Cocktail is cortisol. Cortisol is commonly known as your main "stress hormone." This has always been tied to our fight or flight response and probably a large part of what kept us alive thousands of years ago, back when I was sharing stories in the backwoods of Beaufort County (remember that from Chapter 1?). But here's why cortisol matters to you: It does two very important things to your audience. First, it causes them to pay attention. When my brother and I were running down the hallway and saw my dad holding my mom by the hair, your cortisol levels were spiking and you probably needed to know what happened next. This is that "sitting on the edge of your seat" feeling you get in movies. But the second important thing cortisol does is cause your audience to remember the story. Tension increases memory. You probably don't remember every good incident you've had driving down the highway, but you undoubtedly remember when that guy cut you off and you had to slam on breaks to narrowly avoid a collision. Same thing. Understanding how this hormone works, and how to create it, in the minds of your audience is crucial if you want your story to stick.

But the final hormone in the Storytelling Cocktail—the one that really puts you over the edge and gets you drunk on stories—is oxytocin. Oxytocin has historically been known as the "love hormone" as it is elevated in our brains when we physically connect with other humans, like in a hug. When a mother is breastfeeding her child, for example, oxytocin is through the roof in both of them, which is one of the reasons it's such a bonding moment. But the reason it matters for your brand storytelling is that oxytocin is also created when people feel and understand what someone else is going through. It creates a deep feeling of empathy. In Dr. Zak's experiment with Ben's video, the levels of oxytocin in the brains of the research subjects were dramatically elevated. Watching Ben, knowing his illness was terminal, and his father who was struggling to accept it, hurt the audience as if it was their child. But empathy is not enough to inspire action. The real impact of oxytocin and the empathy it creates, however, is that it causes people to trust those in which they empathize.

STORYTELLING COCKTAIL

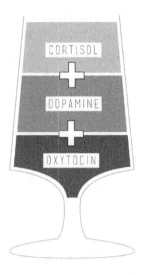

Dr. Zak explains further in his *Harvard Business Review* article:

> As social creatures, we depend on others for our survival and happiness. A decade ago, my lab discovered that a neurochemical called oxytocin is a key "it's safe to approach others" signal in the brain. Oxytocin is produced when we are trusted or shown kindness, and it motivates cooperation with others. It does this by enhancing the sense of empathy, our ability to experience others' emotions. Empathy is important for social creatures because it allows us to understand how others are likely to react to a situation, including those with whom we work.

So now you know that when we earn each other's trust from sharing stories, it isn't just the knowledge that we aren't in immediate danger of being harmed. There is actually a neurological force at work, telling us that this person is good, so we drop our guard and begin to trust them. And once we trust them, we care enough to want to learn more about them. Empathy, as you'll find, is the key to connection, and connection is key to conversion. And if you use storytelling in the right way, you can make that initial connection of what hopefully blossoms into a long term client relationship.

PUTTING MONEY WHERE YOUR TRUST IS

Dr. Zak's experiment didn't end with just finding out that certain hormones were elevated in the brains of their subjects when they heard a good story. In the next stage of their study, they brought in a new variable: the almighty dollar. After playing the same video about Ben, Zak and his team gave the research subjects the chance to share money with someone in the lab. Those who produced oxytocin were more likely to donate their money generously to a stranger they couldn't see. In a second experiment with money, they gave people the chance to donate to a charity that works with terminally ill children and the same result happened—those who released oxytocin donated money to the charity. Not only that, but the amount of oxytocin released predicted the amount of money people would donate to either a stranger or a charity. Zak's lab soon partnered with the Defense Advanced Research Projects Agency (DARPA) to measure not only blood, but heart rate, skin conductance, and respiration. And they could predict with 80% accuracy who would donate money based on the levels of oxytocin in their brains after watching Ben's video. What all these experiments proved is that a story can actually change someone's behavior patterns by altering their brain chemistry. If you're trying to inspire your audience to take your call to action, whether it be buying your product, or downloading your lead magnet, or simply visiting your website, do you think storytelling might help you achieve that? I hope that question is rhetorical by now. When you get someone drunk on the Storytelling Cocktail, and you give them somewhere to direct that euphoric energy, they will take that action.

I decided to put this to test myself when an opportunity organically rose in my work. A while back, I was running a crowdfunding campaign for my feature documentary, *Finding Croatoan*. By this point, I had conducted successful crowdfunding campaigns as well as some that failed miserably, so I felt like I had a pretty good grasp of what worked and what didn't. Telling a story worked. So when I found myself just $400 shy of our $3000 goal, then quickly knocked back even further by a technological mishap while shooting, I propped my iPhone up on my laptop screen, cut on the video camera, and told the story to my followers. It went like this:

"David and I just got back from an awesome weekend of shooting in the Outer Banks, but Saturday we woke up and it was just like a torrential downpour, a monsoon. So we were like, 'Right, well today's a wash. Get it? (wink) We're not going to get anything accomplished.' So that's a bummer, you know, that's what we came down here to do. We only had two or three days. But about 2:00 or 3:00 in the afternoon, the sun came out and the skies opened, so we were like, 'Uh, let's go to Hatteras and get that drone shot! We got to at least get something done today.' So we packed up the drone, drove an hour and a half or more -- we were staying in Kitty Hawk --

get to Hatteras, pull over, get the drone out, and launch it. It gets about 15 - 20 feet in the air and it comes crashing down onto the concrete. Here is the camera -- broken into many, many pieces.

And so we were just like, 'Okay, well now today is really a bummer.' Yeah, so sometimes this happens. We didn't hit anything. It was in a clear area. I think just one of the rotors malfunctioned and it just came crashing down. These are the perils of filmmaking. Technology! Like, sometimes stuff happens and it did happen this weekend. We are less than $400 from our goal in this campaign and here we are now going to have to replace this. So it is literally sometimes one step forward and two steps back and now more than ever, we need your help. If you haven't donated, click the link below to our Seed & Spark page and please give anything that you can and it literally will go to the drone first and then we can get back and try to raise the money to finish the film. We couldn't do this without you guys and we're so excited to tell this story. Thank you so much. We definitely need your help, now more than ever. But either way, we will prevail. Thanks so much guys."

Within just an hour of releasing that video, we received over $750 in donations and it sent us past our goal with plenty of time left in our campaign. People that had wanted to donate, but hadn't found the time yet were motivated to finally do it. And others who maybe weren't sure about donating were now inspired by our tenacity and donated. And others still that didn't even know of our project, empathized with our plight and donated money, too.

I used this example in a video storytelling workshop once and asked the audience what they noticed. One person responded: "It was so real! And the tension of this thing happened, then this happened -- we were right there with you and we wanted to support that cause."

Whether she realized it or not, she was responding to the science of storytelling. "We were right there with you." is narrative transformation and neural coupling. "And the tension of this thing happened, then this happened" shows her increased levels of cortisol and dopamine. "We wanted to support that cause" shows empathy and increased levels of oxytocin.

I know you didn't get to see my charming face on the video, so you missed my wink when I said "Get it?" You also didn't get to see the broken drone, which I held up as proof. But even so, what stood out to you about that story? Do you think you would have donated?

One last thing you'll learn from Dr. Zak about the science of storytelling is that since my video actually told a story, chances are you might donate. But if I didn't tell a story and just went on camera asking for more money, you almost undoubtedly would not—unless you were my mom, in which case you better always donate to my fundraisers.

Zak's team, still partnered with DARPA, took the experiment to one final level. In the next version of the study, they used function brain imaging (fMRI) to measure the regions of the brain that were activated while watching Ben's cancer video. They then compared those readings to a control video, which featured Ben and his father walking at the zoo, passing random animals. What they found is that the most active areas for the emotional story were areas of the brain associated with understanding and empathy and areas that had lots of oxytocin receptors. However, the control video that just had 100 seconds of Ben and his father at the zoo did nothing. None of those areas of the brain were activated and the audience blanked out. To elevate those Storytelling Cocktail hormones in the brain and induce empathy, the video had to have a narrative arc for the research subjects to follow.

This is why you need to learn how to tell stories effectively *before* you learn the tools with which to tell them. The tools will always change, but the way stories work in our brains will not. It has been that way for humans since my caveman counterpart was in the backwoods of Beaufort County and I believe it will remain that way for us humans, even as we see technology play a more dominant role in our society. Like what separated us from animals in the past, stories will separate us from machines in the future.

And even though to tell a great story you must be in touch with your heart and all those warm fuzzy emotions inside, it is all backed by the brain. There is an undeniable science behind how stories work and what makes them great and there is a certain structure you can follow, no matter what medium or format you use, to tell them effectively.

Now that you know *why* storytelling works, you are ready to learn *how* to put it into action.

Chapter 3

THE UNDENIABLE STORY STRUCTURE

When I competed in my first story slam that January night at The Monti, I won because of multiple reasons. Yes, my story made the audience laugh as well as cry, and yes, the tension of the sequence spiked their cortisol, so they would remember it. But I also won because the judges grade each story on the structure of the story itself. And mine was damn near perfect.

So what is a good story structure? Many of the folks that I competed against in the story slams were excellent performers and their stories were certainly entertaining. But if they were loosely ranting about the theme of the night, the whole time running off towards hilarious tangents, they weren't really telling a "story." They were just talking about a topic. The first thing that makes a story a story is simple -- so simple, that it is most often overlooked. A story is made up of three parts: a beginning, a middle, and an end.

There are many different approaches to story structure and many different formulas to follow, but they all come back to the same basic shape—the story arc. Most of the time when we imagine arcs, we see them as symmetrical - like Paris's Arc de Triomphe, or at least McDowell's "golden arcs" in the Eddie Murphy classic, *Coming to America*. But a story arc isn't quite designed that way.

I'd love it if people were still reading this book 100 years from now, and if I'm so fortunate for that to be the case, I don't know how this next comparison will age: a story arc is roughly the shape of the Nike "swoosh" logo, if you flipped it upside-down and backwards. It starts low and slowly rises until about the one-third mark, where it then starts rising higher and faster. It continues that trajectory until it reaches the peak of the arc, or the climax of the story, which is generally around the two-thirds mark or three-fourths mark of the story. After the climax, the arc dies off quickly with a resolution. The French would call it the denouement, and their Arc de Triomphe might be the only reference here that people understand 100 years from now.

Even though the structure looks simple, there's a lot going on under the surface. You don't have the time to learn all the nuances of story structure that novelists and filmmakers know. You just need to understand an easy-to-follow formula, and the best way to achieve that is to use the classic "three act structure." It was good enough for Aristotle, so it is good enough for you.

THE THREE ACT STORY STRUCTURE

The best way to think of this is in the three-act structure of a play or even the format that you were taught in grade school for writing papers: an intro (Act One), the body (Act Two), and your conclusion (Act Three).

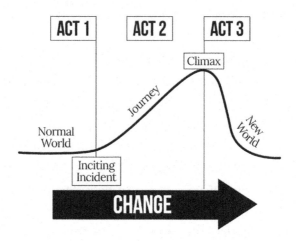

ACT ONE - THE PROBLEM

In Act One, the story begins in a "normal world" where there is some balance. This is the introduction to the character(s) your audience will follow for the story and the world in which they exist. Also referred to as "narrative exposition," the audience might learn background on the people and places, as well as other information that give them context on their existing routine. There is a balance that exists. Life might not be great for your characters, and it may not be terrible, but it is manageable and the characters are content(ish). Balance.

In my story at The Monti, the first act is when Beau and I were always sleeping in his room on Christmas Eve and hearing what he told me was reindeer on the roof. In my crowdfunding video for *Finding Croatoan*, this was the first few seconds when I established that we were down at the Outer Banks to film, but the torrential downpour prevented us from doing any shooting.

Then, towards the end of Act One, something happens that pulls the character out of their normal world and disrupts the balance of their normal world. An external force enters their life and either creates a new problem or forces them to finally face an existing one they've been hiding from. Either way, it creates the challenge that the main character will face and the quest they will take to overcome it for the rest of the story.

This specific moment is called the "inciting incident" and it sets off a series of events that should nail the audience to their seats, waiting on the outcome—at least if it's a good story. For my story at The Monti, this was when my brother and I heard the loud noise followed by my mother's scream. For the *Finding Croatoan* crowdfunding video, the inciting incident was when the rain abruptly stopped and the sun appeared. The inciting incident is when both conflict and opportunity are presented. This moment, in my opinion, is where your story *really* starts. But it's definitely when Act Two starts.

ACT TWO - THE JOURNEY

Once that challenge of the inciting incident is presented, the character must make a choice. Will they face this problem and try to solve it, or will they run from it (hint: even if they try to run from it, they will *have* to face it eventually, or else you have no story)? This is my favorite part of the story. It is what starts off the wild roller coaster ride of Act Two and if done right, should keep

45

your audience glued to the seats after you hooked them with an interesting problem.

In my story at The Monti, Act Two starts when my brother and I run down the hall and turn the corner to see what caused the noise. In the *Finding Croatoan* crowdfunding video, it is when David and I decide to make the 90-minute drive to get the drone shot and hop in the car.

Act Two is the largest part of the story. Some storytelling experts actually suggest that it accounts for fifty percent of the entire story (divided into two parts: Act 2A and Act 2B). This is the part of the story where tension climbs continuously. The character will try potential solutions to the problem that inevitably fail. They may meet a mentor, or guide, to help them along the way. They may meet additional adversaries that knock them off track. The audience will follow this rising action and constant conflict that eventually leads them towards the ultimate climax of the story. There are twists and turns, ups and downs, small wins and setbacks—while the characters face internal and external conflicts along the way.

In my story at The Monti, this is when my brother and I see that my dad is holding my mom down by her hair, her screaming for us to help, and us screaming for him to let her go, while searching for something to help. In the *Finding Croatoan* crowdfunding video, this is when David and I are driving down the two-lane Highway 12, through all these little beach villages, looking out to see if the storm will come back, and prepping the drone to fly.

ACT THREE - THE RESOLUTION

Act Three is the final act and this is when you reach the climax. This is the highest point of tension in the entire story, where the forces of conflict and the characters come face-to-face for their final showdown. The odds are stacked against the character and they must make a final commitment or sacrifice to overcome the obstacle.

In my story at The Monti, this is when Beau is out of options, sees the Wilson tennis racquet, hits my father in the side of the head with it, and bloody chaos ensues. In my crowdfunding video for *Finding Croatoan*, this is when—just as we were about to "win" with our drone flight—the rotors malfunctioned in mid air and the drone came crashing down. *That* story was a tragedy. But take note that we still used it to achieve our fundraising goal because it created empathy in the minds of our followers.

The climax is followed by a small amount of falling action, usually resetting the world the character was in to a "new normal" with a new balance and order to things. Things have changed after that point and the characters should have learned something about themselves, or changed their perspective.

In my story at The Monti, this was sending my dad down the hospital aisle and realizing, through my mom's final words, that our family was living with a secret. In the *Finding Croatoan* drone story, this is David and I coming to the realization that bad things will happen but we must continue to forge forward, and eventually finding a way to turn this loss into a win.

That is the basic structure of a story that you should follow—beginning, middle, and end. Granted, great storytellers can use creative license to unravel stories in a myriad of original, unusual, or exciting ways, but these are the basics. And no matter how far you plan to take your storytelling journey, the basics are the most important skills to grasp. If you are proficient in any area of your life—athletics, academics, music, or whatever else—you know that to get to the point of being advanced or considered an expert, one must master the basics. The best at what they do even know that once they are experts, they must still spend time perfecting those basics. Professional musicians practice scales daily. Basketball players perform countless layup drills and shoot hundreds of free throws. Basic skills in anything are like words in a story. The better you become at using them and the more of them we learn, the better you can put them together in creative ways to tell compelling stories.

I don't expect you to become one of the best storytellers on the planet. You've probably got so much else on your plate, that's not a realistic goal. But what's great is that you don't have to be to make a profound impact on your customer with storytelling. You just need to know this basic structure because that narrative arc (no matter how simple) is the foundation of how humans communicate. And many times, if not most times, simple is better than convoluted and complex. Clarity is your communication is your top goal. Let's use the "KISS rule" (keep it simple, stupid!) moving forward. Don't worry about all the details and just remember this for your brand storytelling. A story is simply these three things: a problem, a journey to solve that problem, and then the resolution of that problem.

Problem, journey, resolution. Repeat it continuously.

Even with that simple three-part structure, it might be challenging for you to fill in the gaps when you're building your storyline. Over the past few years, I've talked to countless storytelling experts on my podcast and in my work to find an easy to follow, "color by numbers" model for marketers. A great template

I found to use to expand the three act model into a more in-depth story structure is this simple eight step formula by improv instructor Kenn Adams called the "Story Spine." Kenn is the Artistic Director at Synergy Theater in California. Most of the improv you may know are quick sketches like in the show "Whose Line is It, Anyway?" But Kenn works with actors to create fully improvised long-form plays. Imagine how hard it must be to perform an hour long play where you and your cast member completely make up all the lines! Well, that's why Kenn had to create a simple structure to keep his actors focused on an overall story framework, even while they were improvising. Fun fact: one of his actors eventually went on to work at Pixar and she brought the formula with her, which Pixar still uses as their story framework today. And I think we can all agree the folks at Pixar are some of the best storytellers on the planet.

The Story Spine goes like this:

THE STORY SPINE

Once upon a time _____

And every day _____

Until one day _____

Because of that _____

And because of that _____

And because of that _____

Until finally _____

And ever since then _____

Since we've already mentioned the *Rocky* franchise, let's go back to that as an example. The first *Rocky*, in 1976, won Best Picture at the Academy Awards, was nominated for 10 of them in total, and launched the long career of now legendary action star, Sylvester Stallone. So it's fair to say it's a pretty good story. The story of Stallone writing the movie is also amazing, but we'll save that for another day. Let's break down the film with the Story Spine. It would go something like this:

Once upon a time there was a low-rent journeyman boxer named Rocky.

And every day he would fight in local Philadelphia club bouts for $50 a fight.

Until one day, he got a call from the heavyweight champion of the world, Apollo Creed, inviting him for a title match.

Because of that, he had to hire Mickey, his gym's manager, as his trainer.
And because of that, he trained like he never had before and got in the best shape of his life.

And because of that, he started to believe in himself and his ability to win.

Until finally, he faced the champ in the title match and even though he didn't win, he went the full 15 rounds with him, a feat which no Creed opponent had ever done.

And ever since then, Rocky was considered a top contender by the boxing community and, more importantly, himself.

Try to fill in the blanks with your favorite movie. It's easy for us to talk about story structure all day, but you only truly learn it when you practice it. You may not get it the first time, but once you do, you'll clearly understand the basic framework to follow. Most great stories follow a simple structure like the Story Spine—one that your audience can clearly latch onto and one that shows what happens over the course of your story.

No matter what the variables are that fill in those blanks, stories are all essentially about the same thing: conflict, overcoming obstacles, and the changes necessary to overcome them. If your story doesn't have an issue to resolve, it is just something that happened to someone. *That* is not a story. A story is "a character had a problem and here's how they overcame it." There are many different iterations of story structure. The Story Spine is just one of them. But *all* stories include one thing: a transformation.

Stories are before/after. Stories are cause/effect. Stories are about transformation.

CHARACTER > STORY

The transformation that the audience follows most closely is not the transformation in the world of the story, but rather the transformation of the character in the story. This takes us back to how our brains mirror the characters in the story because we relate to them. This is why making a bigger statement, or presenting a thesis, through the story of a character is so effective. If, by the end of your story, the character hasn't gone through any transformation and hasn't developed into a better human (or ogre, or mutant, or toy cowboy) then I'm afraid you won't have a story that people remember for very long. In fact, I would argue that without a good character, you won't have a good story at all.

I'm a filmmaker. And whenever I tell someone what I do, they almost always tell me about a "humdinger" of an idea that they are ostensibly suggesting I make a documentary or series about. "I just think the world of craft brewing in North Carolina is so popular right now, it would be a hit. And it hasn't been done yet!" one friend said to me. "That might be true," I replied, "But who are the characters we are following? What's the story?" I then go on to explain that the "world" the show is based in is just the setting. It's the backdrop. Yes, the setting can add a ton of value and even excitement to a story (the beaches of Normandy in any World War II film, the galaxy far, far away in Star Wars, etc.), but it's just the backdrop. A great story is always about the character's journey.

THE CHARACTER'S JOURNEY

- **Who is the character?**
- **What do they want?**
- **What's stopping them from getting it?**
- **Who or what comes along to help them?**
- **How do they end up getting it?**
- **How did they change as a result?**

Reality television has been incredibly popular in the past two decades and it seems like now there is a show about everything. But it doesn't matter if these shows are set in the high-stakes world of fishing for Alaskan king crab, the wheeling and dealing floor of a popular pawn shop in Vegas, or the hustle-hard empire of a music mogul. These shows are about families. They are about arguments and heartache, camaraderie and love. These are things that any family experiences and therefore any family, watching the show on their couch, can relate to. Sitting in the living room, most people in the family watching the show will find someone that they identify with in the show. This makes them want to root for that person or group of people. Having an exciting setting is always helpful, but at the end of the day, what we latch onto are emotions that we have experienced ourselves. We crave that connection. And that connection comes from relating to people—in this case, the character in the story.

So what makes a good character? It's hard to say, actually. It certainly isn't that they are likeable. That could be helpful, but there have been too many characters that are jerks throughout history that people love. In 1990s television, sparked by HBO's hit series, *The Sopranos*, we saw the rise of the "anti-hero." The anti-hero wasn't a new concept in storytelling, or even in filmmaking. Dirty Harry was an ultimate anti-hero and he had seven movies. But in television, when networks needed audiences to keep coming back week after week, there was a long-held belief that the protagonist had to be a good person if the audience was going to root for them to win against whatever foe they faced in that week's episode. What cable television at the turn of the 21st century taught us was that just wasn't true. Protagonists like Tony Soprano, Walter White, Dexter, Nurse Jackie, Nancy Botwin, and Don Draper weren't necessarily "good" people. They were murderers, drug dealers, serial killers, and liars. But, they all had reasons for their misdoings that the audience could somewhat understand. Tony Soprano was trying to provide for his family, as was Nancy Botwin and Walter White. More than that, they had the same struggles as "regular people" and suffered like they do. Tony Soprano was suffering from depression and anxiety. Nurse Jackie was addicted to drugs. Don Draper was running from his past identity. These are issues that people in the audience could relate to. It humanized the characters instead of making them monsters that are purely evil. In short, it meant people could empathize with them, or at least *why* they did what they did. When people are able to see themselves in a character, it opens the door for empathy.

In the second season of my podcast, I spoke with Melissa Cassera, screenwriter of *Girl Followed* and *Her Stolen Past* on Lifetime Network, and she expanded on why we feel this way:

> *You can't have a good story without good characters -- really deep, rich characters. All I write is really complex, messed up women characters. That's what I'm known for here in town, that's what I get hired for. It has to be a character that you're excited to go on a journey with, for whatever reason.*
>
> *If you don't have that piece, your story falls flat. I do not care. If it's plot-heavy or if it's just exploring a world, then that just becomes so boring and there's nothing to actually invest in. We need a human being that we can invest in. And even if they're an "unlikable" human being, like a Tony Soprano character, you're still going to have something that you can relate to with him. He's a ruthless mobster, but yet you relate to him because he's in the pool with the ducks, and he's a dad, and you also see his mom and how he was raised. You can relate to all that. You can relate to the pressure you might feel to keep up with what was expected of you and to get sucked into a family business—regardless if you're a mobster or not.*
>
> *So there's all these elements that come about with a*

character like that that we can connect to and we can see ourselves in and we want to go on that journey with them. So I think that's the most important part of a story. And when I write my scripts, that is all I focus on is character. All my time is focused on that. You can pour plot into it later. Plot is easy. It's the characters that are tough, that a part of that takes a while.[10]

Will Simpson, writer and producer of Netflix's *Myths and Monsters* had this to say during my interview with him about what makes good characters:

> "It's not a question of likability. It's a question of relatability. Look at, say, a myth like Medea. So the story of Medea, it's a mother who murdered her children -- the most horrendous acts you can almost possibly imagine, but in the hands of a great playwright, like Euripides, she is the most compelling character yet you can sympathize with her. You can almost go with her to that point and she can take you there. And yeah, she's one of the the greatest characters in literature for her debt, for her contradictions. But most of all, I think for what she does to her audience, which is to challenge them and to kind of say, "You may think I'm a monster because of what I'm doing or about to do or have done, but what would you do in the same situation?" and how easily we can slip from good to bad, and what does it take for a human to do that? So to me a great character like that, it's not about being likeable. It's about challenging an audience."[11]

If you know that people resonate and empathize with complex, realistic characters, and you know good stories are about change and development within those characters, then you absolutely must learn how to weave those kinds of characters into the structure of your stories. The most classic example, that so many stories still follow, is "The Hero's Journey," outlined by Joseph Campbell in his book The *Hero With a Thousand Faces*. The Hero's Journey has been adopted by filmmakers throughout the history of cinema—perhaps most notably by George Lucas in *Star Wars*—and is broken down simply by Will Simpson:

> "The hero's journey is the name of a theory developed by an American academic called Joseph Campbell, who studied myths and stories from cultures all across the world. And he thought he saw a pattern in those stories. He developed this idea called the "monomyth," which was exactly that, that they were a pattern to these myths told across the world and is specifically about a hero and a hero leaving his ordinary world to set out on adventure—usually on some sort of quest— to find the elixir of life or to find the thing that's going to save his village or whatever you want. Along that journey, he meets various helpers and allies who could be magical, and he meets various foes and he has to overcome various challenges in what Campbell terms, 'The Road of Trials.' And in doing so he sort of learns and grows as a person. The hero then approaches the greatest challenge of the story in which, if he succeeds, he can seize the object of this quest. So when he gains victory and wins the prize that he sought out to seek, he can come home, not just to change his world but as a changed man himself."

Again, there's that word, "change." And if you lay out the journey of that change in a good narrative structure, where you present the challenge or conflict, display the choices made by the characters and the changes that those choices create, you can create a resolution that not only has a lasting impact on your audience, but also one that inspires action.

There is a scientific reason that stories will work for you—they directly alter the brains of your audience. There is an artistic recipe to follow and rich characters that touch the hearts of your audience. But the most important part of incorporating a storytelling strategy into your brand or business's marketing is that stories are the most effective tool in creating human connection. What you do with that connection is up to you and the mission of your business—i.e. grow your community, encourage donations to your nonprofit, promote your products and services, or just build brand awareness.

This book is about video storytelling. But the way that two-word phrase is structured is misleading. Because if we were to talk about camera equipment, lighting, and mobile editing apps at this point, that would be putting the cart before the horse. Or the tool before the skill. Maybe we should call it storytelling video, instead. Remember, the tools will always change. But if you focus on cultivating the skill of storytelling first, then you can use whatever tools you have access to at the time to tell them. And as you go along and get better, you will acquire new tools to tell them better. But the tools won't do the work for you.

Now that you've learned the science of storytelling and the structure of a great story, it's time to put that knowledge into action. This approach is not a tactic that you will use for one part of your marketing. It is an overall strategy of communicating your brand's messages clearly and should be embedded in all of your marketing—internal and external. That means you can use it for video marketing, like we'll talk about a lot in this book, but you can also use the knowledge of telling great stories in your website copy, social media posts, when crafting press releases and secure media appearances, to align your team behind your mission during meetings, while giving speeches, workshops, and presentations, and in so many other ways. And after reading this book, you will be able to put this into action immediately. There is no barrier to entry, no investment needed. You just need to be human, which I'm hoping you are if you're reading this.

Even though we've established a couple of easy formulas to follow, storytelling is not a one-size-fits-all task. There are countless kinds of stories that you can tell. To find the one(s) that will be most effective for you and your business, you must diligently mine for them. They exist deep inside the purpose and mission of your brand and you will need to arm yourself with emotion and empathy to find them. The good news is, stories are happening all around you, every day in your life and business. You just need to learn how to recognize the opportunities to tell great stories when they arise and then seize those opportunities! In the next few chapters, you're going to learn exactly how to do that.

PART TWO

HOW TO TELL GREAT STORIES

Chapter 4
WHICH STORY SHOULD YOU TELL?

So now that you know why stories work and even what a good story is made of, it's time to think about how all this applies to your business. Learning theory and new ideas are nice, but does any of it matter if you don't put it into practice? Time to get tactical.

It took me years to realize how I could take the knowledge I gained during the Raise Up journey and strategically use it to grow my business. Hell, it took me years to even realize what I had learned about myself. That's because I wasn't listening to the story I was telling myself and seeing the potential to change the narrative I had created in my head. But when I finally did, I understood exactly how I could serve my audience like no one else in the world. To set yourself apart from others in your industry, understanding very clearly what you do, why you do it, and how your specific approach differs from that of your competitors is extremely important. But understanding how to clearly communicate that to your potential customers through narrative is imperative.

This leads me to the first kind of story you should be telling: your Self Story.

THE SELF STORY

The Self Story is the story of WHAT you do and how you got there. It's the most important because without that, you will have no idea where you are driving your work and all the ambition built up inside of you. And if you tell this story right, not only will your audience have a clear understanding of what you do and how it can help them, they will already feel like they have a relationship with you. So having an *actual* relationship with you is easy for them to imagine. And that's your goal, right?

As a country boy from a small town in North Carolina, traveling to 20 different countries to make a movie about an urban fitness subculture I was in love with was the best time of my life. But it was quickly followed by the worst time of my life when I was out of money, drowning in debt, and trying to figure out the best way to tell the story. At times I felt completely lost, not knowing if I would ever be able to pull a decent movie out of the countless hours of footage I'd captured. I remember being on my mom's couch in January of 2015—three years since I had started this journey—crying because I couldn't find my way out of this predicament. My belongings were in a storage unit in Queens and I had lost most of my good connections in the New York film community. I was broke so I moved back home, but my North Carolina film community had forgotten about me too, so I was getting no calls for new gigs there, either. I was living off of credit cards, debt was piling up, and it seemed like every day something new was going wrong with my car. It was one of the lowest points of my life and somehow I was trying to create a decent piece of art through it. But I never stopped. I kept getting rejected by film festivals. I kept getting "no's" from distributors. I kept running out of money. But, I also kept showing shitty versions of the movie to test audiences, while working to whittle the film down and get to the heart of the story.

When I couldn't find anyone to distribute the film, my team and I took it on the road and toured it around the United States ourselves. Some screenings would have 60 people and some would have 6, but the effect was always the same. People loved the movie. And people left inspired. Each time we'd figure out a way we could make it a little bit better, based on what the audience reacted to. Eventually, after almost two years of editing, we finally got accepted to a film festival. It was the Hip Hop Film Festival in New York—the absolute *perfect* film festival for this movie. The Hip Hop Film Festival was in Harlem, the birthplace of the movie, as well as the fitness movement the movie followed. The house was packed for our screening, everyone stuck around for our panel discussion afterwards on health and hip hop, and we ended up winning "Best of the Fest," the overall prize of the festival that year. I cried when I got the news, but it was a different type of cry from the one on my mom's couch that January in 2015. Then, in the beginning of 2017, capitalizing off of that success, we sold the film to Red Bull Media House for global distribution on their streaming platform Red Bull TV. This was a storybook ending for an ultra low-budget independent film like *Raise Up*. This put me in a super small percentage of indie filmmakers. Thousands of stories like this are told each year and relatively none of them get seen, much less sold. This became *my* story.

Through the process of making and releasing *Raise Up*, through all the ups and downs, I learned that those qualities I once perceived as flaws were actually my creative strengths in disguise. All I had to do was take my limiting beliefs and reframe them from a different perspective—or in other words, change the story I was telling myself. The only camera rig I could afford on this project was a $1000 Canon DSLR camera and one zoom lens. That was it. I took my camera and a backpack and went around the world documenting this subculture in the most rag-tag, DIY-style possible. There was no support from a production company producing this film, so I had to tackle every aspect of the filmmaking process myself. But if I viewed it from the other perspective, I was the only person that could've done this because I was a part of the calisthenics culture myself and it helped me build the right relationships in the community. Also, I understood the fabric of the culture and could display it in the documentary with authenticity. It might not have been the same with an executive over my shoulder, focused only on budget and timeline. Because I didn't have the nicest camera gear, or even much camera gear at all, I thought it would cheapen the look of the film that deserved to be perfect. But again, if I reframed that thought, not having a good tripod and only having one lens meant that I didn't have time to set up beautiful shots—I had to shoot "run and gun" style and follow the action as it was happening. The shaky handheld footage and quick zooms gave the film a gritty, rough look that was actually perfect for the vibe of the culture. It wasn't a story that needed to be glossy and glamorous. Plus, this made the audience feel like they were right there in the park with the characters, not watching a well-crafted scene from a bird's eye perspective.

Without any money, I also worried about those parts of the film that usually benefited from expensive animation or graphics. That was the content I initially thought I might need to capture the attention of a community obsessed with YouTube highlight reels. For the opening credits sequence, I leaned into my lack of money and went intentionally "lo-fi" with my approach. The new calisthenics culture I was following was born out of hip hop, so I found a graffiti artist, who was also a member of the calisthenics community, to create a mural of the film's title and I filmed the whole process on a timelapse. The opening credits feature clips of dynamic, eye-catching calisthenics moves mixed with the artist spraying paint on a brick wall. The last frame of the sequence lands on a wide shot revealing what the artist was painting: the words "Raise Up" which served as the film's title card. It looked beautiful and set the tone for the film. I'm still proud of this decision and all it cost me was a $400 plane ticket to Los Angeles.

After changing the stories I had been telling myself in my head, I finally learned what it was I had to offer—what made me unique and set me apart from others in my field. People were always so fixated on what camera I had and asking about all the gidgets and gadgets that they should use to make their videos. Sometimes I didn't even know the equipment they were referring to and sometimes they could tell. My imposter syndrome was in full swing during these moments. "Am I *really* capable of pulling this off?" I'd ask myself. Anytime I'd feel them sizing me and my camera up, I'd simply tell them, "I could take an iphone and do more than that camera, because I'm telling a story. Remember, it's the man not the machine...." with a smile and that would shut them up, at least for the moment. At first, my response was a defense mechanism, but it soon became my philosophy. I started viewing all my work like that—focusing on the heart of the story and worrying less about the fluff and extra features. The story had to be solid first the effects were secondary. This is the same process I use now for clients to produce award-winning documentaries. We keep production small and cost-effective, and tell simple heartfelt human stories that inspire their audiences to take action. I had turned my tragic flaw into a superpower.

That concept of turning flaws into strengths and finding opportunity among your obstacles is not unique to me. Generally, people tend to focus more on what they struggle with and eventually can become very skilled at it. Often, those people go on to help others who are experiencing the same struggles. For example, I now help small business owners, entrepreneurs, and nonprofits understand how to tell heartfelt video stories when they don't have a lot of money, resources, or skills—because that's what I had to learn how to do through making *Raise Up*. You might have something that you learned the hard way, too, that you help people through with the service you provide. Or perhaps you created a product that you couldn't find on the market that would've made your life easier. Most likely, whatever you do, it is solving some pain point that you might've experienced yourself. And your unique path to solving that pain point should be what you focus on when telling your Self Story.

Take a long hard look at yourself and your experiences. What is your unique perspective or approach to the work that you do? Why would someone go to you for knowledge or value versus someone else? Why would they believe you? Why would they invest in you? If you want to build your brand, or engage and connect with your audience in a deeper capacity, you need to tell them your Self Story. More likely than not, people will have experienced similar situations or experiences to those in your Self Story. That means they will connect with it and therefore connect with you. And that is the first step to converting them to customers or clients.

Being different is better than being better. And your Self Story is one thing that will always be different from anyone else's in your field.

THE SERVING STORY

Your Self Story shows "WHAT" it is you do. For example, after reading my Self Story, you now know that I help clients create inspiring videos that don't require a lot of crew and money by keeping production simple and focusing primarily on the story. The next story in your arsenal will be the Serving Story and it shows "WHY" you do what you do.

I struggled with my Serving Story for most of my life. Growing up, I had many different interests, but the two I was most involved in were athletics and the arts. But it was hard for me to let those two worlds intersect, because when you grow up in eastern North Carolina, or probably any rural community, people tend to identify you as one thing only. Who knows if that's how they really were or if I just created that in my head, but either way I kept my two worlds, and the people in them, in different compartments. I thought my jock friends would think I was a "wuss" or too sensitive if they knew how much I loved Phantom of the Opera and knew every song, and I thought my artistic and nerdy friends would think I was too much of a meathead if I talked about how Emmitt Smith was the greatest running back of all time. I became a chameleon, but I never really felt comfortable being my true, multi-layered self.

I fought this duality for much of my childhood and had no idea which path I'd choose as an adult. But when I accepted I wasn't going to be a professional athlete, I went to college for Media Production and focused on film and television production. After college, I spent five years studying under documentary filmmakers and working as a production assistant on TV shows. I did anything I could to make money with a camera—from wedding videos, to sports recruiting videos, to shooting live concerts of my friends' bands. But I still felt pulled to the world of sports and fitness, so in 2007 I started boxing. I competed for a year or so and eventually began instructing a boxing fitness class at my local gym. That led to me becoming an assistant coach for the boxing team of the University of North Carolina. I quickly learned something interesting. It was almost as fulfilling teaching someone a skill, watching them apply it in the ring, and winning their fight, as it was when I won my fights. I received (almost) just as much joy. But I experienced zero percent of the punches to the face. I was happy with those odds and retired from my short boxing career to teach more.

I spent my days working on building my video production business and at night I went to the gym to teach class or campus for boxing practice. Since I had to create new routines every class, I found myself searching for new and interesting exercises on YouTube. That's when I found freestyle calisthenics. Visually, it had the flow of boxing, or even breakdancing. People were doing pull-ups and push-ups, but they were doing them with style. It was an art form. I started incorporating these movements into my own training and then into my classes. People loved them. I'd also fallen in love with the culture of freestyle calisthenics, which was rooted in a social movement aimed at bettering the lives and health of the area's youth. This movement had heart. It had a story. And I wanted to tell that story.

All the videos I saw were based in New York City—in either Harlem or Brooklyn—and as fate would have it, I'd move there in 2010. I found myself in a unique position to marry my two passions: filmmaking and fitness. I spent the next few years documenting this underground culture as it rose to the mainstream and started spreading globally. I followed this movement around the world and back and it consumed my life. Then I moved back to North Carolina in 2014 to finish the movie. It was harder than I thought, especially being the sole driving force behind this monumental task with all odds against me. I struggled for the next three years.

Fortunately, I found a new home to explore my love of fitness during this time when I was hired by a fitness studio to teach circuit classes. I showed my classes the bodyweight exercises I had learned and they loved them, too. My video production jobs were few and far between, so I made fitness my main focus. I hosted health and wellness events, tried to get fitness parks built in my hometown, and created lots of workout content for social media. It was all tied to the promotion of *Raise Up*, which was a good thing, but the imbalance between my athlete and artist identities was significant. Some people thought I was a filmmaker as a hobby, and a personal trainer as my profession—when, to me, it was really the other way around. This did damage to my ego.

After we finally sold the film, I made it out of "the pit" I was in when I was dead broke, depressed, and watching my debt grow. But I wanted to be taken seriously as a filmmaker and I wanted the world to know that I could create other heartfelt stories that didn't have anything to do with push-ups. I had been so immersed in the calisthenics world for five or more years that I wasn't sure how to break out the mold I had created. I toiled back and forth on whether I should just marry myself to being "the fitness guy" or if I should create the type of art I knew I was capable of making. I felt like a squirrel in the middle of the road—unsure of which side to dart to before the car runs him over. Here I was, twenty years later still fighting the same fight with my athlete/artist duality. I even worked on two new film projects in the fitness space that, although they weren't my own projects, I put all my hopes and self-worth into. Though I had no control over it, they both failed and I felt more lost than ever.

This required more soul-searching on my part and I employed the help of many friends, mentors, and coaches. A lot of it hinged on my own ego, insecurities, and control issues. I had to ask myself, "What is *really* bothering me?" So what if other people thought I was "the fitness guy"? At least they thought *something* of me. At least I *had* stories to tell. Plus, there's nothing wrong with trying to spread the knowledge and love of living a healthy lifestyle. That's virtuous, right?

I started to really think about what mattered to me. I asked myself what my core values were. I thought about where I came from and what experiences made me who I am. I looked at what work I had done that had been successful. Years earlier, I was nominated for two Emmys for healthcare documentaries. My longest running client was the Neuroendocrine Cancer Foundation, which probably single-handedly kept me able to pay my mortgage at times. *Raise Up* wasn't the first project I had done in the world of health by a long shot. Something kept bringing me back to the same concepts, whether in my creative work or my client work.

Furthermore, I was raised in a part of the country where heart disease, obesity, and cancer were prominent. My father was an alcoholic that died of lung cancer, my cousin died of cancer, and both my mom and brother are diabetic. Health was *important* to me—not just physical health, but the other pillars of health that are so intertwined with our physical health. Stress, anxiety, depression, and addiction ran deep in my bloodline. Finally, the light bulb went off in my mind. My mission became clear. I wanted to tell stories that helped underdogs navigate those different pillars of health. That was the perfect intersection where all my unique skills, passions, and experiences met. Once that mission became clear to me, I could make it clear to everyone else. And showing people the purpose behind my work demonstrated my core values and in today's world of business, what you stand for is just as important as what you sell.

The best way I have found to connect with people is to show them what your purpose is. I think the world has moved to a place where business and entrepreneurship has a "values first, profit second" approach. Or at least where they're both 50-50. You can see this shift over the past few years with terms like social entrepreneurship, corporate responsibility, and purpose-driven business. People are genuinely trying to make the world a better place, and I think that having a social mission as part of your business is going to be an integral part of its success or failure. And the way to communicate that social component is through this story.

When you are crafting your Serving Story, you have to open yourself up and be vulnerable. It ain't easy. A lot of my coaching and consulting clients equate it to therapy and they're not wrong. To understand why you ended up doing the work you do (and there is a story there), you have to dig up a lot of your past and previous experiences. I liken to how you put together a jigsaw puzzle. If you were to just pull one piece of the puzzle out at a time and try to put it together, you'd never finish. So instead, what do you do? You dump all the pieces out on the table and spread them around so you can see them all. Then you start to see corners and end pieces that connect, and eventually pieces that are the same color that connect, too. And after a while, the image starts to emerge. It's the same thing with your unique experiences. You have to look at ALL of them, even from when you were a child, and after working for a while you can start to see the intersections of your skills, passions, and experiences, and put them together in a very specific way that paints a beautiful picture of who you are and what you were put on this earth to do. Think small. Think specific. A business who wants to serve or sell to "everyone" can't really help anyone. Telling your Serving Story will help you establish *who* it is you seek to help, *why* it is important to help those people, and *how* you intend to do it.

Most of the time, people don't hire you for your expertise. They hire you for your unique perspective on the work that you do because they think that approach or philosophy will help them. And that is directly derived from the life experiences that have informed and influenced the way you view the world. So share that story. People will connect with it, I promise.

THE SUCCESS STORY

If the Self Story tells your "WHAT," and the Serving Story tells your "WHY," then your Success Story tells the story of "WHO" it is you help. This is one of the most effective stories to tell if you are trying to sell your goods and services or get donors to support your cause. However, it is sadly still overlooked by most companies and organizations who are still stuck in the habit of touting their accomplishments in order to raise interest in what they provide. If you look at most websites these days, they have one video on the homepage talking about how amazing they are. Even if they use other people (i.e. testimonials) to say it, all the video is saying is how great the company or organization is, just in a variety of ways.

Like I mentioned earlier, I've worked with the Neuroendocrine Cancer Foundation for many years. Their mission is to increase awareness and educate the general public and healthcare professionals about neuroendocrine tumors (NETs), to support NET cancer patients and their families, and to serve as patient advocates. Neuroendocrine cancer is a rare disease that is often misdiagnosed as a gut condition—like Crohn's Disease or irritable bowel syndrome—or undiagnosed, which can cause it to be fatal. If it is diagnosed early, however, it can often be manageable and along the lines of a chronic condition versus a deadly disease. NECF is a small foundation with big goals. On the home page of their site they claim it boldly: "We will have achieved our mission when everyone worldwide is aware of Neuroendocrine cancer and neuroendocrine tumors. Until then, our work is not done."[10]

When we first started working together, the foundation had done very little video but they knew they needed to pivot in that direction to keep up with major nonprofits. It was 2011 and they had decided to create a six-part series that included videos like: The ABCs of Neuroendocrine, Surgery and Treatment for NETs, Lung Neuroendocrine, and Living Well with NETs. All of these were data-driven videos that were well-received in the community and quite successful for the foundation in terms of viewership. Granted, when their previous view counts rarely surpassed 100, there was only room for improvement. The videos carried out the part of NECF's mission that sought to support patients and serve as patient advocates, but they didn't increase awareness or educate the general public. One of the videos, "Faces of Hope" tried to focus on patients' personal accounts with the disease but it was merely a montage of different soundbites or segments of stories. It wasn't cohesive and it didn't draw the viewer into a narrative. It wasn't a story. I take blame for that. I should have educated my client and coached them on a better way to reach people. But I wasn't the storyteller then that I am now. Six years later, we had the chance to do it again, and I wouldn't make the same mistake.

NECF wanted to do another series of videos in 2018, but this time to honor their 50th Anniversary as a nonprofit organization. The original idea was to create more of an update to the 2012 videos—focused on new treatments and developments. But when the sponsor mentioned wanting to do "human stories" that were full of hope, I urged the foundation to agree. I told them that while they were more generic and not as informative, they would actually do a better job of achieving the overall mission because they would reach many more people. In the previous videos, we were basically "preaching to the choir," or speaking to people who already knew about the disease and were searching for more information. That was a good service to provide, but if we told heartfelt stories that resonated with more people, it would increase the "shareability" of the videos and therefore impact more people. Then we could give those who wanted more information access to it, by offering a call to action to visit the website (or subscribe to their YouTube channel, or sign up for their newsletter, etc.).

In 2018 the foundation launched its biggest video campaign in it's 50 year history—a twelve-part documentary series, with me at the helm. The videos told the stories of how patients emotionally and psychologically navigated this rare cancer diagnosis. Each video followed the story of one person, or one family, and focused on a different universal theme—like love and intimacy, work, parenthood, faith, friendship, family, and healthy living. Because people that didn't have the disease could still relate to those universal themes and the characters featured in each episode, they could then be moved and inspired by the personal stories of overcoming a life-threatening disease. This allowed the series to be more successful than the foundation ever expected.

NECF didn't include any content about themselves, even when the subjects of the film's mentioned the foundation in their interviews. (This is called "branded content" and is another valuable type of video to use in your brand storytelling.) The focus was not self-serving, but rather on serving those that the foundation sought to impact: patients and caregivers in the neuroendocrine cancer community. What's most important, though, is that *because* they focused on telling great stories of inspiring humans and stayed true to their mission, the results of the campaign worked wildly in favor of the foundation. The campaign amassed over 100,000 views, and an over 800% increase in video views on their Facebook page, their biggest platform. Their number of followers grew over 15% in that year, proving that they were reaching a new audience, and their FB messages increased 100% (this is actually my favorite stat), showing that they were creating the direct engagement with the community that they desired. Moreover, they were recognized by the marketing and advertising community by winning two Communicator Awards as well as their peers in the healthcare industry by being nominated for two Sharecare Awards (which is kind of like a healthcare Emmy Award). Though they didn't win a Sharecare Award, sitting in the audience listening to Dr. Oz present each award among companies like Pfizer and Johnson & Johnson, and organizations like AARP, American Heart Association, and American Cancer Society, the message was clear: NECF was now playing in the big leagues.

If you have helped any of your clients play in the big leagues, land a new client, improve in any way, or overcome any obstacle that has left them in a better place in their lives, then you need to tell those stories! When you tell your Success Stories, you are taking advantage of the opportunity to reach people in a completely new, and more meaningful, way—one that is being neglected by most of your competitors. To put it simply: your business or organization is not about you. It's about whom you impact.

In Chapter 3 we talked about "The Hero's Journey." Often, brands view themselves as the hero, from a first person point-of-view. It's natural to do that. But in the Success Story, you are not the hero— *your client* is. You are the guru that will lead them to their "new world." You are Obi-Wan in *Star Wars*. You are Gandolf in *Lord of the Rings*. Isn't it clear now? You are a wizard! And only your wizardry ways can help people out of the muck they are in and send them off to succeed on their quest.

Think about when the guru comes along in the quest. He or she appears right when a conflict or a big choice arises in the hero's journey. Where is that point of conflict for your customer or audience? This is where you want to start when crafting your Success Stories: what problems do the people you serve have? Then, you just simply tell the story of how you will help them solve those problems. The guru leads the hero into the "new world" which is unfamiliar and, quite often, scary for the hero because of the new environment and challenges that arise. In *Star Wars*, Luke has never been off his desert planet of Tatooine, where he lived on a farm. His journey soon included big cities full of gamblers, criminals, and thugs—the hardships of hyperspace—Wookies, Tusken Raiders, a Diagona in the trash compactor, and whatever species the bounty hunter Greedo was—the power of the Force—and the omnipotent Empire lead by Darth Vader (this all may be a bit too esoteric if you haven't seen the original *Star Wars*). The whole movie is a string of near-death experiences and if it weren't for Obi-Wan leading Luke along, he would have quickly been overcome in any of these situations. You are Obi-Wan.

Think about how a guru would talk about themselves. Are they narcissistic, or are they humble and prefer for the focus to be on the hero? Have you ever heard someone talk about all their accomplishments before? It's annoying. Imagine this: you and I meet at a conference after-party and I say, "Hi! I'm Rain Bennett. I'm an international filmmaker that's been nominated for Emmy awards and produced work for The Travel Channel, The Weather Channel, and Red Bull TV. I've been interviewed by Men's Health and I've written for The Huffington Post. It's been a roller coaster ride, but man, it feels so good to do what I love and get paid well for it. I'm actually very successful. Did I mention I once flirted with Maya Angelou in her North Carolina home? Anyways let me know if you guys need help! I can definitely create social media videos for you that would make your organization blow up." How quickly would that trigger your gag reflex?

Alternatively, imagine the scene went like this: you, my client June, and I meet in a bar at a conference and talk about what we do. I tell you I'm a documentary filmmaker that works with businesses to create emotional, impactful short videos when they don't have huge marketing budgets. Then I go to the bathroom. While I'm gone, you ask June how she knows me and June says, "We actually met at another conference. I saw him speak and he was talking about *exactly* the things I needed help with at my nonprofit. I told him what we do and what we were struggling with and he helped us come up with a long-term video marketing strategy that ended up saving us money *and* increasing our donations. Plus we got nominated for two awards, which our corporate sponsors loved! But really, I could tell he was super passionate about what he does and who he works with. He walked me through the whole process and over-delivered every time we worked together." If you needed help with storytelling or video marketing, which one of those situations might lead you to want to work with me more? I know you understand this in your heart. But time after time, people's heads tell them that they have investors, donors, or board members they have to please, so their storytelling efforts just focus on the numbers. They talk about how many people work for them, why their purpose or product is so important to the world and how much effect they can have, and, most importantly, how much all this will cost. Testimonials are businesses' historic attempts at the Success Story. But the overwhelming majority of these have fallen flat, either by just talking about the business, or failing to tell a story. If you scan homepages of the internet right now and see examples of these testimonials, you'll generally find sound bites like "ABC Corporation changed my life with their product!" or "XYZ Charities is one of the most important foundations in the world and that's why I support them with a monthly donation!" Sure, we all know what the purpose of a testimonial is: to show your audience other people that have received benefits from your product, service, or cause, in an effort to gain sales or support. But the key here is to be subtle. Put the shine on your customer or community and tell *their* story—of which your company or organization merely plays a role in (albeit a profound and pivotal role). The way to craft a Success Story that has maximum impact is to weave yourself into their narrative, not to dominate it.

THE BEHIND-THE-SCENES STORY

Now that we've discussed how to tell the What, Why, and Who of your business in a story format, let's discuss "How" you do it all. That's right. We're going to show the people how the sausage is made. I can hear your heart starting to beat faster. "What?" you ask, with that eyebrow of yours raised. "But I thought a magician never reveals his secrets! And I thought what they don't know won't hurt them!" Historically, perhaps people may have not wanted to know how the proverbial sausage is made and much preferred to just pay for it and enjoy its deliciousness conscious-free. But here's what happened. Businesses started taking advantage of people, lying to them, and manipulating them into buying things they didn't want, need, or that were actually bad for them. And the consumers found out. Now, they are sick of being lied to. People are craving honesty and authenticity more than ever and if you are empathic enough in your business, you can give them what they need and still achieve the success you seek. In fact, it may be the key to the success you seek.

We talked about a great example of this in Chapters 2 and 3 when I told you about the crowdfunding campaign for my film, *Finding Croatoan*, and the video update that pushed us past our goal. Remember the story about the drone crashing? Well that definitely helped push us over the edge, but it certainly wasn't the only reason our crowdfunding campaign was successful. It was a proven tactic that we had used before, so I knew that it would be effective. The campaign where we lost our drone was actually the second crowdfunding campaign we'd run for this film project. Its goal was to help us get some final interviews and finish production. The first crowdfunding campaign was the one that got the project off the ground—which is often more than half the battle. In the first campaign, we raised $10,000 and learned all the "dos and don'ts" of crowdfunding. That's how I knew that when the drone crashed, it was a perfect opportunity to flip our adversity into an advantage by telling the story.

If you aren't familiar with crowdfunding, it's basically a way for individual donors to contribute to your project, product, or idea, instead of traditional investors, grants, or credit cards. The creators offer different packages that donors can choose as contributions in exchange for various "perks" or prizes. But the "pitch video" is where the creators explain exactly what they need, why they need it, how they're going to use it, and what the donors get in return, in a convincing enough way to get people to reach into their pockets and send them cash to carry out their plan. When my co-producer and editor David and I launched the crowdfunding campaign for our new documentary, we were already fighting an uphill battle. Although we were proven filmmakers at that point and our last film had won awards and received global distribution, we were completely new to the worlds of archaeology, history, and adventure—in which our new film existed. We didn't have a foot in any of those cultures and we were newcomers. We needed to penetrate these communities to get people excited enough to donate to our project and we had to think creatively. Fortunately, I *did* have a significant foot in the "eastern North Carolina" world—the setting of our documentary—since I grew up there. That meant I already had a following established from friends and family. Plus I knew what mattered to the community. So for the pitch video, I leaned into that and told a version of a Self Story that expressed why I was so interested in this subject and why I was the best person to make this film. All North Carolinians grew up learning about "The Lost Colony" of Roanoke Island and when I mentioned that it was the childhood connection to the story that drove me to make the film, it resonated with other people who grew up with the story.

Our pitch video did well. It received 30,000 views, and for a small indie documentary trying to raise just $10,000, that was significant. If one-third of those viewers donated just *one dollar*, then we'd easily have our goal. It wasn't that easy, though. The video got eyes on our project, which was a good thing, and it even brought in our first round of donations, but it wasn't enough to reach our goal. We thought about what else we had that would excite people and convince them to donate. Then it dawned on us. People wanted to be part of it. And if they couldn't be there with us, the next best thing would be for them to feel like they were. David and I had exclusive access to the dig site of the archaeological team we were filming, which was literally kept a secret from everybody except their team and various media channels like History Channel and Travel Channel. So, without giving away our location, we decided to tease out little behind-the-scenes videos to let people in on the secret.

The platform we chose for this was Facebook Live. It was perfect because it played right into the authentic, spur-of-the-moment feel we wanted to create. We wanted them to feel like they were standing beside us. The first live video we did was on Day One of the dig. We gave people a little peek at the dig site, educated them on what a "midden" was (an old dump for domestic waste) and why we were digging there, and told them what to look forward to. People engaged immediately. Comments "This is a really exciting project!" and "This is so awesome! I've been reading about this." popped up and then the snowball effect happened. We realized this was too good of an opportunity and extremely cost-effective for the conversation it created, so we made it part of our campaign strategy. Daily, if we could, we'd check in via Facebook Live to show our followers, now growing by the day, any new developments. We were careful not to show the same time of content too often (like the dig site, for example), lest people get bored. We never wanted them to feel like it was a video they'd already seen. In one video, we showed them a few of the artifacts found by the archaeologists and volunteers, in another we educated them on the process of peeling back the layers of time in the dirt, and I even played to their sensibilities by including my mom in a video. As I mentioned earlier, my family and the whole community back home was interested in this story, so my mom joined me on one of the most important days of filming—where there was a community debate between competing camps of archaeologists trying to find The Lost Colony. On the way back to our rental cottage, I threw up the camera in the car and my Mom and I discussed our thoughts on the debate via Facebook Live. And no, I have no shame about using my mother to get donations.

Our following continued to grow from sharing our Behind the Scenes Stories. We had consistent engagement and interaction with the community we were building and before long, we had reached our goal and our crowdfunding campaign was "greenlit"—a filmmaking term that meant we got the go-ahead to start our project. Fortunately for us, we had already started, so this gave the support and foundation we needed to carry our film to the next stage. More valuable than the financial foundation the campaign gave us was what we learned from it all. People want to feel special. They love things that are exclusive and only a select few people get to experience. That's why people pay more for VIP backstage passes at concerts. It doesn't make the music sound better. It makes them feel special. People want to see behind the curtains because it makes them feel like they are a part of the experience, instead of just a witness to it.

But there is a caveat. For many creators, telling a Behind the Scenes Story puts them in a vulnerable position. Businesses and brands want to seem like they have ultimate confidence in what they're doing and/or creating. They might not want to let the audience see what's happening behind the scenes. Because what's actually happening behind those curtains is a team of frantic people running around making mistakes, barely holding the operation together, and desperately hoping no one finds out things are falling apart at the seams. Why would anyone want to show that to the public? Well, the answer is: no one does. But if you lean into that fear and allow yourself to be authentic and vulnerable, people will empathize with your journey and want to be a part of it. And because they empathize with you, they'll be rooting for you to win. So let them into the VIP section. Welcome them. Then they will become loyal followers because they are also a part of your story.

One great brand that has embraced the Behind the Scenes Story is Social Media Examiner, a company that helps people "navigate the jungle" of social media. SME hosts a top podcast, provides loads of free content on their website, and also has a yearly conference called Social Media Marketing World. In 2018, owner Michael Stelzner had a bold idea. He wanted to grow his attendance at the conference from around 3000 people (the previous year) to 5000. But *that* wasn't the bold idea. He proclaimed his goal on video for the world to see. But that wasn't the bold idea, either. He decided to create a behind-the-scenes show that would follow his team on this quest, through all the ups and downs, mistakes and mismanagement, trials and triumphs. He called the show: "The Journey." It was a simple documentary-style show, produced and edited by one team member and released every week leading up to the conference on YouTube. Social Media Marketing World 2019 ended up getting 4800 attendees (just 200 shy of their bold goal), but along the journey (see what I did there?), their YouTube subscriptions increased to about 30,000 and "The Journey" had hundreds of thousands of views, and they still got their conference attendance up by 60%. I'd say their vulnerability paid off well.

Think about this in your own work. How can you make your customers or clients feel special like they have their own backstage pass to your business? Your video marketing should always do one of three things: entertain, educate, or inspire. And if you do a Behind the Scenes Story well, it can do all three. As social media evangelist Gary Vaynerchuck says, just "document, don't create." If you do it well, it will deepen the impact on your current superfans as well as bring new supporters into your sphere to root for you.

THE SAGA STORY

The fifth story you should be telling is a Saga Story. The Saga Story is a story on your brand or business's historical timeline—you know, your saga! The Saga Story tells the "When" you made the What, Why, Who, and How happen. The great news is, no matter how old your business is, you have a historical timeline and that timeline is full of ripe stories to pick. Just remember that it's not just any moment you are looking for, but rather a story of a significant moment where things changed for your company or organization. You have to "show, not tell" your audience the message you're trying to convey to them by telling that story.

The most common Saga Story is probably an origin story (also known in some storytelling circles as a "founder's story"). This is a good one to start with because everyone's business had an origin and it probably happened because of a problem that needed to be solved. We all love a good origin story—just look at how many there are for our favorite superheroes. But so often, businesses miss other great opportunities to connect with their customers through other stories on their historical timeline. You could tell the story of how your business responded to some event (e.g. the housing marketing crash) or disaster (e.g. showing hurricane relief work you took part in). Just make sure that it is sincere and aligned with your business's values and not just pandering or capitalizing on something that has caused people pain. You could tell the story of when you reached your fundraising goal, of when you had your first breakthrough, or when you booked your first big client. But don't forget that even though this is a story about you or your company, the message lying within the story should still target your audience.

To me, one of the best Saga Stories is a story of rebirth—not about when your business was "born," it's about when you were reborn and set upon your new and current path. It's the story of when you flipped the script, turned your fears over on their heads, and used them as stepping stones. It's the point of no retu.... okay, you get the picture. You had a life before "the moment" and you have a new life afterward. This kind of story is even more popular after the Covid-19 pandemic of 2020 because almost every business experienced a huge transformation—even if one of growth—when the world shut down. I can't tell you how many events I spoke at since then that have had the theme of "revisioning" or "hitting reset," or "how to pivot." If you can tell this story properly, it will show what you stand for as a brand as effectively as any story in your arsenal.

My favorite Saga Story is my mom's. Her whole life she wanted to be a real estate agent. She had an affinity for houses, especially historic homes, in eastern North Carolina and was a natural born salesperson. She talks a "mile a minute" with a southern accent and a smile that can defeat any hard negotiator. But she had a problem. My father was one of those men who was threatened by his wife seeking any kind of life of her own and he wouldn't let her go to school to get her real estate license. She still worked at H&R Block during tax season and also as a substitute teacher throughout the school year (much to the demise of my privacy or any cool factor I was working on). So apparently my dad allowed her to contribute something financially, as long as she didn't get too "big for her britches." (There's a lot of Southern slang in this book, I hope you're keeping up.)

Finally, she left my dad, an abusive alcoholic, after two decades of trying to make it work. Once they separated, I guess my dad's masculinity was even more bruised, and it took years for us to get any kind of financial support from him. Fortunately, my mom inherited a house from her parents, but that's all she had. So we cobbled together furniture from mostly thrift stores or gifts from friends. She and I spent the whole summer of 1998 renovating the house ourselves. To this day, I can still smell the moldy dust coming out of the 30-year-old green shag carpet we ripped up off the floor and stairs. I can still hear the sounds of "oldies" soul classics and picture painting the house while listening to the radio on my boombox. Even though we were struggling to make ends meet, my mom saw the opportunity to finally go for her dream. No one was there to stop her. And even though a sales job wouldn't see immediate payment (she had to actually *sell* something first!), she still felt that it was her destiny.

So she got her license and found a job at the only company that would hire her—a super small independent agency in the neighboring tiny town of Bath, North Carolina. Even though she was competing with much more recognized franchise companies, she won "Rookie of the Year" in her county and became known as a force in the local real estate scene. After a few years of success, she was ready to fulfill her dream entirely and start her own company. She partnered with another woman in 2005, when the housing market was at an all-time high, especially with the waterfront property that my hometown had in abundance. Because my mom and her new partner had already been successful in their real estate careers, this move was threatening the existing "establishment" in the local market. The owner of one company, which had dominated the real estate scene in Washington for the previous 30 years, said to a colleague, "those little girls won't last six months."

My mom and her partner found an office just on the outskirts of town and cobbled together a rag-tag team of agents that didn't already belong to a company or were inspired to leave their companies and join what was then called Coastal Rivers Realty. This disruption of the status quo was not normal, and frankly not taken lightly, in a small-town market like Washington's. So Coastal Rivers Realty made a bold statement with their slogan claiming that they were "Making Waves in Eastern North Carolina." I'm still very proud of her for that line (it tells a story all on its own!). When Coastal Rivers Realty's office opened, they hardly had any furniture and their phones were on the floor, with cables and wires stretching from wall to wall. But they were nine agents that shared a common dream—to break the mold and create a company that truly sought to serve their customers. To incentivize the team, my mom and her partner made a bold goal. They wanted to get 30 listings in 30 days. They got it. They bumped it up to 60 listings in 60 days and this time they made their goal public. They got that, too, and the town started cheering for them. So they took it even further and made the boldest goal they could think of: 90 listings in 90 days. Not only did they achieve it, but they blasted past it with 100 listings in 90 days! They took out an ad in the local newspaper and said "Thank you, Little Washington, for 100 Listings in 90 Days!"

Since then, Coastal Rivers has become a Coldwell Banker franchise, survived with only two other companies through the housing market collapse of 2008, opened three other offices, and overtaken the 30-year reign of the previous leading company by consistently outselling them for the past four years and gaining 42% of the market share. All of this has been because of one decision they made back in 2005: to always put the customer first in any of their efforts and successes and have sincere gratitude that the community allows Coastal Rivers to serve them in their home buying journeys. My mom knows the power of this story and she tells it to customers all the time. It touches on so many classic storylines that we love. It's a "rags to riches" story, it's David versus Goliath, it's a story of rebellion against the status quo, and one of empowered women taking control of their lives. When she tells it to potential customers now, they immediately feel inspired and confident that they are working with a company that won't let them down. They buy into the story. And then they buy a house.

If your Saga Story is told well, it should have hints of all the other stories embedded within it. You should be giving them a peek behind the scenes, where they understand what it is you set out to do, can clearly see the purpose that is driving your mission, and most importantly, identify who you are trying to impact in the world. At their core, stories are all about making tough decisions to overcome one's fears or obstacles. Your Saga Story gives you a chance to show the moment you decided to stand up to your fears. That's what will make people believe in you.

Don't make the common mistake of thinking you have to tell your brand's whole entire history in one story. That is most likely impossible, without it requiring a 10-part series and probably boring your audience to death. Go back to what you learned in Chapter Three about the structure of stories and find any moment along your historical timeline with a problem, journey, and resolution. The thing is, stories are happening in your life and work every single day. They might not all have deep meaning that make them worth telling to your customer, but they are still happening and many of them *will* make an impact. The sale you made today is a story. The new product you launched this month is a story. The increased revenue due to that new marketing campaign is a story. Each and every moment is a chance to tell a Saga Story that shows your evolution as a person and as a business.

Are these the only kinds of stories you can tell? Of course not. There are an infinite amount of stories you can tell and myriad ways you can tell them. The stories in this chapter are just frameworks to get you started. As you've already heard me say, the number one rule in storytelling is to show, not tell. These five examples of stories are perfect ways to *show* the Who, What, When, Why, and How of what it is you provide people.

Nowadays, you have the ability to tell stories in almost any situation. There are so many tools out there that you can use. This doesn't just apply to video storytelling, this applies to audio storytelling, written text, images and photography, and even face-to-face when you're speaking to somebody. Any time you have an opportunity, no matter the medium, to tell someone a story about a project that you're doing, the mission of your organization, or a customer that you've helped, take it. Remember that the point is not to boast, but to show the person or people listening what it is you do like no one else and whom you impact with your work. This is how you make them understand what your purpose is and how you plan to impact them next.

Stories aren't things that you make. They are things that you take from real life scenarios and then mold into lessons learned that you can use to help others. Not every story needs to be told, but the ones that can evoke emotion and show a path toward transformation absolutely should. And they are all around you, every minute of every day. My job is to help you see the opportunity to tell those stories and your job is to *seize* those opportunities to help more people.

But like any artist, seeing the opportunity and having the inspiration to create is not enough. Then the time comes when you have to sit your butt down and do the work. You're going to make mistakes along the way. But you're also going to get better. Way better. You just have to start. You are armed with a heart that feels emotion and a brain that thinks of amazing ideas. That's all you need to start. But eventually, you're going to have to pick up some new tools.

Chapter 5
THE TOP STORYTELLING TOOLS

So far we've covered a lot about what you need to do (tell stories!) and why you need to do it (they inspire people to take action!). And if I were like the rest of the storytelling experts out there, that might be all that I tell you to do. So much storytelling content is just about high-level theory and looking at this as a marketing strategy from only the 30,000 foot view. But I'm not like everyone else. I'm special! Or at least that's what my mom tells me. The way I would word it is that I'm "different." Many of my storytelling peers and contemporaries come from big name brands like Pixar, Google, Facebook, Apple, or are Hollywood producers and filmmakers—all with big budgets and full teams to help them create great video stories. They aren't small business owners or nonprofit directors or solopreneurs with the world stacked against them like you are. You need to know how to tell great stories when you're just starting out and have a lack of resources at your disposal, not how to do it with million dollar budgets. My background is in low-budget independent documentary filmmaking. You can't get more grassroots and ground level than that. My perspective on storytelling is the tactical, boots-on-the-ground information you will need to survive and later, thrive. I truly care about you taking this advice, applying it, and maximizing your impact on the world. Stories are not just a marketing strategy for your business. They are a way of communicating and connecting with humans. They are *the* way to communicate and connect with humans. And storytelling is just as important of a life skill as being able to read and write.

So for the remainder of the book we are going to talk about the most important part of storytelling for your business: how to actually do it.

In 2021, you have more options of where and how to tell stories than you ever have before. I want you to see that this is an outstanding opportunity. But for many people, with the gift comes the curse, and having so many options actually presents problems for them. They ask themselves, "Where do I even start when it comes to my storytelling efforts?" and often that question remains unanswered and therefore their stories untold. Even after reading the first four chapters of this book you may be like, "Cool, Rain. I know a lot more about stories now! But I still don't know what to do on Monday when I need to create content. How do I actually do it?" If we first take a bird's eye view at what your options are, and look ahead to your future goals in the next year, quarter, month, or week, then you can make a strategic plan on which stories to tell, which tools and tactics to use, and on which platforms to distribute them. You already understand the heart of storytelling, but now it's time to use your head to make the decisions needed to implement them in your business and marketing strategy.

The first kind of storytelling that ever developed was live, in-person, around the campfire stories. "Campfire" makes it sound like a Boy Scout camp, though. These were fires that the community congregated around to not freeze to death, cook whatever food they could find, and fend off predators. These fires were much scarier. Let's instead call them Life-or-Death fires. Luckily, the early humans had stories to keep them busy and lighten the mood. Language is widely believed to have started around 100,000 years ago. And my guess is, stories came soon after. As you've already learned, this was a way for people to communicate with each other to earn each other's trust. Then, they'd know if they were friends or foes, and trade if they were friends (or perhaps roast marshmallows by the Life-or-Death fire), or fight if they were foes. Storytelling was how they shared their common early human experiences and kept track of their history. Later, this is how epics like Homer's *The Odyssey* were created—by oral storytelling. Later still, this is how I won my first storytelling competition at The Monti.

Me and Homer. Just two guys telling stories around the fire.

A BRIEF HISTORY

After tens of thousands of years of humans just making weird sounds with their mouths, the game changed. We began to create images. Historians and archaeologists argue why humans first began to draw their experiences, but sometime around 40,000 years ago, they started "painting" and carving images on the inside of cave walls. Most specialists argue that this wasn't, in fact, just humans trying to set their creative selves free—bored with the monotonous 9-to-5 lifestyle of hunting and gathering—but rather an attempt at communicating and expressing thought. They might have been even trying to (dare I say?) share stories with each other! Studies have shown that cave art may have been the earliest version of creating language. One linguist from MIT noted, "*Our research suggests that the cognitive mechanisms necessary for the development of cave and rock art are likely to be analogous to those employed in the expression of the symbolic thinking required for language.*"[12]

Our communication and cognitive abilities evolved just as our physical traits did. Picture art soon became symbols representing words and evolved into the earliest form of what we know as writing. The two earliest forms of writing are Sumerian cuneiform (3500 BCE) and Egyptian hieroglyphics (3200 BCE). And although cuneiform is widely known for its wedge-like impressions in clay to convey word concepts, early linguistic systems (like hieroglyphics) started as pictographs, or images that signify what they resemble. Pretty soon, people got tired of having to crawl into caves to read their favorite stories and yearned for a more mobile version of this new thing called "writing." Basically, they were searching for their version of the e-book.

The Sumerians took their cuneiform script and applied it to clay tablets. Soon after, the Egyptians started using papyrus scrolls. A couple thousands years later, the Greeks (arguably history's greatest recorders) took their more complex writing system to parchment. In the early years of the current era, the Chinese invented paper and in 868 AD and the first book was printed on it. Then, in the mid 1400s, a German goldsmith made a breakthrough that would impact the world to this very day. Johannes Gutenberg created a metal alloy moveable type (the Chinese and Koreans had created other moveable type systems, but they never caught on) as well as the printing press that he used it on, and printed around 180 copies of The Bible. Gutenberg's invention is widely regarded as the most important event of the modern era and spawned a printing revolution around the world in the 1500s. The fact that you are reading this book right now, no matter if it is it's printed version, audio version, or e-version, is because of what he created—the most valuable storytelling tool of the next four centuries.

After a couple hundred years, newspapers were invented and their publication shot up with the increase of literacy in the early 1800s. But in 1826, the game took another leap forward when the first photograph was taken. By the late 1800s newspapers started including them with their printed text. Around that same time, several people and inventions led to the invention of motion pictures and in 1895 the Lumiere Brothers showcased scenes of people walking around Paris in public demonstration of their invention, the cinematographer. Just eight years later, the first narrative film "The Great Train Robbery" was shown, with an actual plot, and cinema as we know it was born. Around the same time (what an era!) in the late 1800s/early 1900s radio was created—a new way to broadcast audio, but instantly around the world. In the 1940s we took that sound and added pictures to it and created broadcast television. Decades after television, we created the internet, where we could communicate with anyone in the world at any time. Now we have websites, blogs, social media, streaming video, podcasts (wait, we're back to radio?), AR, VR, AI, and probably tomorrow some other acronym for how we can just send images directly to each other telepathically.

Like the turn of the 20th Century, we're now in an era where new communication and storytelling tools are rapidly emerging—this time at a pace we've never seen before. You have myriad options of how to tell your stories as well as places and platforms to share them. But at the end of the day, you still tell stories by using some combination of either words, sounds, or images. So let's take a look at each of those tools and how you can use them to tell better stories.

VISUAL IMAGES

"If a picture is worth a thousand words, then a video has to be worth at least 1.8 million words."
-Dr. James McQuivey[13]

Dr. McQuivey takes a very mathematical approach to this analogy, literally multiplying 30 pictures, or frames, a second—a typical video frame rate—by 60 seconds (the length of a typical "explainer video" and coincidentally the maximum video length for an Instagram post in 2021). Even though this number is very specific and dependent on a video being a certain length, you get the point: a video is worth many more words than a single picture. For the sake of organization/clarity, I'm going to combine video and photography in this section and just treat them both as "visual images." Photography has been used for storytelling for about 200 years, but for the purpose of keeping with our definition of a story—one with a beginning, middle, and end—let's focus on still images as part of a video sequence, rather than isolated images. Granted, good photographs can be powerful on their own (and the great ones can and should tell a story), but most of their use today is in digital media, and usually complemented by text, which tells the story of the subject or subjects in the photograph.

The photographs and videos that are the most effective in conjuring up that empathy that marketers seek in storytelling, are the ones of real people—simply because when we see them, we are looking at people who look like us. Essentially, we are looking at people that remind us of ourselves (this takes us back to the neuroscience we learned in Chapter Two, remember?). One time in my dad's attic, I found a bunch of old photos of my redneck ancestors from the 19th Century and none of them knew what to do to pose. Some were looking off in other directions, most of them had their arms stiffly stuck to their sides, and *nobody* seemed to think it was important to smile. Imagine living in the late 1800s and seeing a picture of people for the first time. Really imagine it. That had to be mind blowing. You'd be like, "How am I holding this thin little piece of paper with these people in it? Why aren't they moving?? That is why some indigenous cultures think that photographs will steal their souls. Is that true or did I just get that from the 1986 movie *Crocodile Dundee*? Either way, I'm sure photographs mesmerized people. They still do. In 2010, an app called Instagram launched that was a social media platform just for pictures. I remember seeing it and being turned off because I had no idea how to navigate it. Facebook *had* pictures, but they also had posts, and "About" sections, and people posted links to articles you could read. Instagram was just pictures and I didn't understand how we could keep up with our friends and colleagues just through their pictures. After a few years and seeing how people were sharing their journeys in the calisthenics community during the filming of *Raise Up*, it became clear I needed to learn fast. (Also, in a quick flash forward: Instagram announced in 2021 that they are now deprioritizing still photos and are considering themselves primarily a *video* platform, to compete with new video apps like TikTok. Does that tell you anything about why this book is necessary to help you?)

The original platform that made video its top priority was You-

Tube. Some people might not consider YouTube "social media," especially since it is the second largest search engine behind Google, but in the early days it definitely was social. Many of the characters in my film *Raise Up* launched their careers off of that platform, and watching how they used it taught me a lot. People are even more fascinated with video today. It is by far the most effective of your potential storytelling tools.

One reason is simply because your eyes are your most active sense. About 70% of your body's sensory receptors are dedicated to vision.[14] So something that catches your eyes' attention, is way more likely to grab your brain's, as well. But a less obvious reason video is the most powerful storytelling tool is because of its ability to synthesize oxytocin just as effectively as telling a story face-to-face with someone. Remember that oxytocin is the key that unlocks empathy, and empathy is the secret to building connections with people. Also, do you remember Dr. Paul Zak, from Chapter 2: The Science of Storytelling? His team proved this and he wrote about it in *Harvard Business Review*:

> As social creatures, we depend on others for our survival
> and happiness. A decade ago, my lab discovered that
> a neurochemical called oxytocin is a key "it's safe to
> approach others" signal in the brain. Oxytocin is produced
> when we are trusted or shown a kindness, and it motivates
> cooperation with others. It does this by enhancing the
> sense of empathy, our ability to experience others'
> emotions. Empathy is important for social creatures
> because it allows us to understand how others are likely
> to react to a situation, including those with whom we
> work. More recently my lab wondered if we could "hack"
> the oxytocin system to motivate people to engage in
> cooperative behaviors.
> To do this, we tested if narratives shot on video, rather

than face-to-face interactions, would cause the brain to make oxytocin. By taking blood draws before and after the narrative, we found that character-driven stories do consistently cause oxytocin synthesis. Further, the amount of oxytocin released by the brain predicted how much people were willing to help others—for example, donating money to a charity associated with the narrative.

When I started my filmmaking career, we were just exiting the era where only professionals could afford or operate film and video equipment. Now, everyone has access to extremely high quality video equipment and it's getting smaller, cheaper, and easier to use every day. Business creatives, entrepreneurs, artists, hobbyists, and even professional creators all use the same video tools now. So the only thing that can really separate you now from a professional video creator or filmmaker, is your ability to tell great stories with those tools. Anyone can buy a nice camera, but not anyone can connect with the hearts of their audience and deliver a clear message that stands out among their competition. That's what I want you to focus on when using video.

What often happens, though, is that people with less experience creating content or less knowledge and interest in learning about video equipment, become overwhelmed by all the options that are now available. Because of this, they do the worst thing possible: nothing. You cannot afford to make that mistake. But a second problem is that some people are so fascinated with new video technology and passionate about creating, that they can often be so wrapped up in seeking each new gidget and gadget that is produced, they spend all their time chasing "the next big thing" and less time focusing on the depth and impact of the material that they are creating (remember talking about this back in the Introduction?). That is putting the cart before the horse and wasting the opportunity to capitalize on the real power of video. If, however, you focus on building the skill of storytelling, video can be the most powerful tool in your toolkit. Whether it is because of optic stimulation or oxytocin synthesis, one thing is certain: no storytelling tool captures attention, resonates with people, and gives you the ability to maximize your impact like video.

Perhaps that's why 1.9 billion people are expected to use internet video by 2021 and video will represent 82% of all internet traffic.[15] Think you should use it to tell your stories?

AUDIO

Many content creation experts say audio is just as important as video. But any decent sound mixer will tell you that it's actually *more* important than what people see on the screen. That's why my audio engineer Mike is always yelling at me to get the microphone closer. If you want to test this, all you need to do is watch a movie that isn't shot super well. Maybe the camera is shaky or out of focus at times, or the visuals are just mediocre and uncreative. The audio in this movie, though, is spot on—it's clear, it's loud, and there's no background noise. In this case, eventually your mind will adjust to the video and you will notice it less, or even chop it up to a creative decision. Then, watch a movie that is properly shot and produced and the video looks amazing, but it has crappy audio. The dialogue is off-mic, there are random pops and hisses, and a lot of background noise. It will reduce that well-polished movie to amateur-hour almost instantly. You won't be able to shake it and it'll be so distracting that you won't be able to focus on the story.

Even though our vision dominates 70% of our sensory receptors, none of our senses communicate with our brains faster than our sense of sound. But, how is that possible, you say?[11]

The speed of light is 299,792,458 meters per second and the speed of sound is only 340.29 meters per second. How can hearing be faster? Well, what's out there in the world doesn't matter to us. It's all about how our brains perceive it (Which begs the age-old question, "If a tree falls in the forest and no one is around to hear it, does it make a sound?"). Once the sound hits our ears, it only takes 0.05 seconds for our brains to process that it received some information and determine what it is. For sight, it takes 0.2 seconds. That's four times faster! This is why we use a gun to start races, instead of a flash of light. Sight is what we've dedicated most of our brain's attention to—the flashy superstar sense that catches our attention—but sound is the quiet, humble workhorse that actually processes more and is more important to the team. This is probably because back in our caveman days, we didn't walk around the woods with our iPhone flashlights leading the way. Once the sun went down, we were in the dark unless we had a fire (and even then it was limited). So hearing a sound quickly, like a leaf or branching cracking, could literally mean the difference in life or death. Are you picking up what I'm putting down? Audio is important.

When I'm working with my editing team on a project, one of the hardest parts about seeing the clear path to telling a complete story is when we are watching the rough cut. We can't do much audio work (like adding music or sound effects) until we have "picture lock," which means no more changes to the visual story. But it feels so incomplete at that stage it's hard to know if the story, or even the scene we're looking at, works. There is clearly something missing. And the ability for music to glue the pieces of a story together and fill in gaps in the audience's mind is never more apparent than watching a film without any. If you watch a pivotal scene in a movie, you may not even fully notice the effect the music is having on that scene. But if you take it out, immediately that terrifying monster becomes less scary, that romantic moment loses its spark, and that dramatic stand-off just becomes two people staring at each other.

For the purposes of storytelling, audio comes in a variety of forms. It usually breaks down into three big categories: music, sound effects, and dialogue or voiceover. All of them are vital to the delivering of information and all of them function as their own storytelling tools at times.

MUSIC

Music seems to have been a storytelling tool since time immemorial. Take a moment to think about your favorite movie scenes. How many of them include a song that makes the scene memorable? For me, it's all of them. Sometimes, just a good visual with the right musical track says more than we ever can with words. That's because music is so good at conveying feelings. Even music without lyrics can convey happiness, fear, sadness, excitement, tension, despair, love, hate, victory, defeat, and so much more. We're able to play games like "Name That Tune" (or "Beat Shazam" or whatever today's generation's equivalent of it is) because just a few musical notes are all we need to make a lasting connection in our minds.

SOUND EFFECTS (SFX)

Sound effects are another powerful tool in the audio storytelling toolbox. What you hear when someone stomps their foot on a bleacher, or when we see glass shatter, or a dog opens his mouth abruptly when a mail truck drives past, is largely already decided upon and expected by the brain. If you heard something different than expected, like human laughter when the dog opened its mouth, you'd be completely baffled (but damn, that would be hilarious). Sound effects are such a normal part of your everyday life that you probably don't even notice them, until they aren't there. Similarly, when I'm recording an interview for a documentary and fighting against some background noise—say, a siren or some construction going on—it can be completely distracting when it's "off-camera" and the audience only sees the person talking on screen but not the cause of the background noise. However, if I were to cut away or zoom out to show the construction worker working, the audience's minds accept it and they can go back to listening to the interviewee speak, without the background noise being so distracting. We just need that connection in our brains. Knowing this, you can see how sound effects can be used as storytelling tools to enhance the experience.

VOICEOVER AND DIALOGUE

The human voice might be the most powerful (and popular) audio storytelling tool. When radio was replaced by television, the business definitely took a hit, but it wasn't completely replaced as many people thought it would be. I think this is because of the performance of the disc jockeys in creating "shows" and delivering music to the people along with a large slice of entertainment, thus building communities and followings. People gravitated to the personalities they liked best and there was an increase in "talk radio" where radio personalities discussed popular topics and current events, but no music was played. The era of "shock jocks" like Howard Stern made this format more popular. Even with the rise of the internet and people being able to stream any song they want at any time, radio keeps hanging on by a thread and a lot of that is because of the people whose voices have become so trusted over the years.

Now we have myriad ways to explore audio storytelling. The advent and rise of the audiobook is a clear example of this. Even though the percentage of people who listen to audiobooks is still lower than those who read e-books (20% vs 25%)[16], it has been on a steady climb since 2016 while e-book readership has stalled and even declined in that same amount of time. This is most likely due to: 1) the rise in availability, and 2) the convenience of being able to "read" while driving, working out, cooking, etc. What's more impressive, however, is the rise of podcasts. Podcasting gave anyone the ability to essentially create their own radio show and broadcast it to the world. As of 2021, there are over two million podcast shows and over 48 million episodes. Over 50% of people in the United States of America have listened to one and 37% of the population listen to at least one podcast per month.[17] While much of what marketers say would have us believe that everything must become shorter to sustain attention in the digital age, podcasts have proven that theory wrong, with some single episodes being upwards of four hours. And some fictional series, like *Serial* from This American Life, stretch their stories out over several episodes, much like a typical television series. Podcasts have reached a point of ubiquity and some would say even oversaturation. But the point is clear: the demand to listen to people that have something to say is there.

This demand has shown itself in a new audio format, just recently gaining popularity in 2021. The only-audio app Clubhouse exploded on the scene at the end of 2020 and beginning of 2021, most likely as a result of the pandemic, with people being stuck and home searching for connection. But the app provided different topic-based "rooms" where users could enter and listen to conversations going on (think: panel discussion at a conference). They could stay a passive listener or raise their virtual hands for a chance to contribute to the conversation or ask a question. It was a brand new way to learn and deliver one's messages. And it became so widely popular that Twitter created its own version, "Spaces," and Facebook created "Rooms" as a response.

MOTION GRAPHICS

As I established early in the book, I am not a technical person and therefore I have never been a technical filmmaker. I go for the heart of the story and the hearts of the audience, so I tend to neglect bells, whistles, and other flashy devices that are good for capturing and keeping the attention of my audience. I try to let the art and science of my storytelling do that. Also, let's keep it real. I'm just not good at it. I initially sharpened my storytelling blade because I was never good enough at using the technical tools to add them to my toolbox. So it was a defense mechanism, but then my style and philosophy developed from that. However, the ubiquity of computer generated graphics and animation grows every day. You don't have to be super technical and you don't need a ton of money to use them. Everyday people—you and I—have access to the technology to add animation and motion graphics to our content.

Ever since 2004, when my Video Production professor at NC

State, Jim Alchediak, told us that motion graphics would be a good field to go into, I've watched his prophecy come true. To be fair, he didn't have to be Nostradamus to see that. Motion graphics had been around for decades already. But with the rise of the internet and the declining barriers to entry with video production and nonlinear editing, being a motion graphics specialist was an increasingly common career path. Alchediak even brought in a former student to guest lecture who was then working in LA in motion graphics to tell us all about the work he did. I still wasn't sold. I was the kid who sat four inches in front of the TV watching HBO at five years old. I was a kid running around the woods with imaginary friends and imaginary storylines. I wanted to be a *storyteller*. And I couldn't do that with graphics. Could I? If I'm being perfectly honest, I didn't really even understand what they meant when they said "graphics." Maybe you feel the same way.

So what does it mean, exactly? It's derived from the Greek word *graphikos*, which means something written, drawn, or engraved, and is used to inform, illustrate, or entertain. It can refer to actually using a graph to illustrate data, and it can also be used to describe something that is overly vivid (like a sex scene or violence that is "too graphic"). Simply put, something "graphic" is something visual.

Well, that was a lot easier for me to understand. In this case, our cave art that we discussed earlier in the chapter are actually graphics. And as someone who believes wholeheartedly in the power of imagery, this helped me understand how I could use graphics to tell my story better. For me, they serve as a way to complement the video and audio—to add something else that will hook the audience into the story that you are telling. This could be a flash of light or color to bring the eyes of the audience to a particular part of the frame. This could be extra emphasis on a motion you, as the storyteller, want the audience to experience (think: an explosion when your brand logo drops down). This could also be a way to take a boring list of data and make it easy to read and more visually appealing. In my work for certain organizations, I use a lot of infographics. Sometimes they are bullet points, product features, or metrics, and sometimes they are step-by-step "how to" infographic guides, like when I show a potential client a "story map" they should follow when building their brand story. It's a way to make it easier for people to visualize the information.

One of the most commonly used versions of motion graphics, since the beginning of motion pictures, is 2D and now 3D animation. Disney is probably the biggest name that comes to mind when you think about animated movies, going all the way back to 1937's *Snow White and the Seven Dwarfs*. But in the 1990s and early 2000s, Pixar changed the game with computer generated animation in movies like *Toy Story*, *A Bug's Life*, and *Finding Nemo*. Disney later acquired Pixar in 2006, so I guess, yeah... still Disney. My big Hollywood friends often use CGI ("Computer Generated Imagery" to use 3D computer animation to add special effects, and sometimes even whole characters, to their live-action film or television stories. Special effects CGI has come a long way, but if you go that route, just make sure your audience actually wants it. Seeing Jabba the Hutt digitally added into the original *Star Wars: A New Hope* in the Special Edition released in 1997 is an example of "just because you *can* do it with CGI, doesn't mean you should." I'm clearly still upset about that. But I'm not alone.

Regardless of potential bad choices that can be made by directors, animation is a powerful storytelling tool that many more people have access to now. I'm seeing corporations and organizations using it in their marketing videos with great success. One of the reasons they can be so powerful in telling a story is because we can do certain things with animated characters that we can't do with real people. Animated characters can do things and say things that real people cannot. This can be used for humor's sake (such as mature audience cartoons like Comedy Central's *South Park* and Netflix's *Bigmouth*), but it can also be used to conjure up empathy and tell sad stories like immigrant children being separated from their parents, when using a real child might not be an option. And that is what animation really provides you: new options for how to tell stories.

People often use what's known as GIFs (which stands for "Graphic Interchange Format") in emails and social media communication to add a little funny to what they're saying. GIFs became hugely popular once Facebook integrated them in 2015 and Instagram allowed users to add them to their Stories beginning in 2018. Sometimes people even use them as a way to increase engagement, like asking a question on Facebook and requiring the responses from people to be with "only a GIF." It's no surprise that engagement skyrockets on these posts because it's simply much more fun to find a three second animated loop of Will Ferrell and John C. Reilly from *Step Brothers* saying, "Did we just become best friends?? YEP!" instead of someone just typing "I agree." as a response to a post. And though the argument over how to pronounce the acronym phonetically (is it "jif" or "gif"?) will probably last forever, they've given us a cute and funny way to add flavor to our social media posts, emails, and text conversations.

Like anything, telling good stories is all about how you use the tools you choose. Can some people throw graphics on their content because it's trendy and hope it'll do the work for them? Of course they can, and they do. But can people also use them as a way to more quickly establish a connection with their audience, grab the attention of who is viewing their content, and even make their stories more powerful? Absolutely. And they do.

But at the end of the day, people relate to, empathize with, and respond to other people best. So if you're using motion graphics, my best advice would be to use them to add to the experience of the strong human connection you're already establishing, or use them to tap into real human interests, experiences, and stories by personifying them (like in animation). Your audience can feel the pain of a lonely cartoon aluminum can that was thrown in the landfill instead of recycled like the rest of his friends, but only because we, as humans, can relate to that feeling of loneliness. That's a human emotion. And your graphics should still play to them.

TEXT

"What has been will be again, what has been done will be done again₁there is nothing new under the sun." - Ecclesiastes 1:9

As we discussed earlier, the Sumerians first created a form of "writing" by using what are called pictograms—images and symbols that represent physical objects. Over five thousand years later, pictures are still the best way to convey meaning. But if you can't use pictures, then the best way is to use words that make pictures in your audience's minds. The structure of any story, in any format, is first shaped by its writing. But in a world that asks creators to "show, not tell," how can you utilize text in meaningful ways that add to your stories, but don't lose your audience's attention?

Historically, people consumed their text stories through books, articles, and personal letters. But in the age of digital media, those were replaced (or more precisely, supplemented by) e-books, blogs, social media, and emails. All of these remain powerful ways to connect and engage with your audience, if you utilize them in the right ways.

E-books have massively reduced the barriers to those wanting to self-publish their books and have allowed a whole new population of writers the ability to get their content (both fiction and nonfiction) out to the public. Having this ability has even shifted the mindset and goals behind writing a book. It used to be a dream of most authors just to have a finished book, and that was the product they were offering. But now the e-book itself can be used as a marketing tool to sell your other products or services. Oftentimes they are used as "lead magnets" for potential customers. Lead magnets are free offerings that creators use with opt-in forms on their websites, so that they then may collect the emails of the reader in the hopes of selling them something in the future. Nothing like free content to get people into your sphere and show them your value before you try to sell them something.

Blogs are another way marketers, artists, and entrepreneurs collect the attention and data of potential customers. More than e-books, which are both fiction and nonfiction, and don't have to have some marketing or sales-based purpose, blogs are usually intended to educate, inform, and (at least indirectly) advertise. Often, like with a free downloadable e-book, a consistent blog about the topics a writer specializes in is used as a "top of the funnel" lead generator. It grabs the attention of a large group of cold leads in the efforts of having them in the writer's sphere and in hopes of being able to sell to them in the future.

One of the most common places to build your list of leads using text is social media. The captions and descriptions of your social media posts provide you with another powerful opportunity for storytelling with text. If you post an amazing picture of yourself casually staring off into the distance at some tropical destination, you might have a text caption that describes where you are, your mood, or what is going on in the picture— even if that text is just the hashtag "#blessed." In today's "Too Long;Didn't Read" era of social media, it's a common belief that little to no text accompanying your content is best. I disagree. If you are telling a good enough story, your audience will come along for the ride, no matter how long it is. You should not, however, ramble on and on with your words. Your content needs to be as long as it needs to be and not a bit longer. At the time of this writing, we are actually seeing a rise in certain influencers and entrepreneurs learning the value of storytelling in their posts. They might post a silly picture of their dog but then tell a story about companionship in the accompanying caption. The engagement on these types of posts show that storytelling works (at least if you know how to do it well). One thing is for certain: just posting a caption like "Me on vacation last week!" or "Spoke at a storytelling conference today!" aren't cutting it. It is important that you have great visuals (nothing can really make up for a bad photo) first, but if you really want to get the most out of your posts, you need to spend more time and attention crafting a simple story that conveys the meaning or purpose of that post. That is where the true value lies.

E-books, blogs, and social media are all great for your top-of-funnel marketing. But one of the best ways to use text to take your audience further down your funnel is through email marketing. This is a prime opportunity to use your storytelling skills. But you have to be terse and pithy with your content in this case. People don't like a lot of text in their emails—that's available to them in your e-books and blogs. Instead, telling a short story that illustrates the point or theme you're trying to convey is the perfect way to make use of a little space and your audience's little time. Show them the value that you have to offer them (specifically through the solutions to their unique problems) and then show them the action they need to take to get your help.

A completely different way I use text in my video storytelling is actually a callback to the early days of motion pictures. Before "talkies" became popular with the release of 1927's *The Jazz Singer*, people watched movies with no sound. Silent movies! Can you believe that, kids? Most filmmakers were presumably good enough storytellers that the audiences could pick up what they were putting down just through the actors' performances, but they had one more tool that helped fill in the gaps in the story: text. Periodically, there'd be a title card that came onto the screen with a background that looked like theater curtains and text of what a character might be saying at the time, or a line that segued into the next scene. Other common ways to use text in films and videos have historically been in title cards like the opening title and name of the production, scene and location headings, lower-third titles (this is when you see someone's name and title below their image during an interview), the closing card with a call to action, captions, credits, and subtitles.

But since 2015, Facebook and other social media sites started autoplaying videos on a user's newsfeed (presumably to get the creator more "3 second video views") and even though they experimented with having the sound automatically on in 2017, most people view these videos with the sound off. This created an issue for creators whose videos were dialogue-heavy. But, like any creative restrictions, it also opened up another opportunity to be creative. You can let the video and pictures convey the feeling of your story, but have text come onto the screen to lay out the structure of your story. This has quickly become a popular format to use on social media and is quite an effective storytelling method.

In 2018, North Carolina suffered historic damage from Hurricane Florence. I was hired by the American Red Cross to create a social media campaign to thank their volunteers for Giving Tuesday. I used this method to tell that story. Here was the script for a 10-clip, 60 second video:

> *September 14, 2018, Hurricane Florence makes landfall in the eastern Carolinas.*
>
> *10 trillion gallons of water dropped in five days.*
>
> *7200+ volunteers and staff mobilized.*
>
> *126,000+ overnight stays provided.*
>
> *330,000+ relief items given out.*
>
> *1.5 million+ meals and snacks provided.*
>
> *100% of it was possible because people came together to help one another.*
>
> *Thank you to all our volunteers.*

When I added that text to images of people in shelters, homes destroyed with furnishings scattered around the yard, and, most importantly, people hugging and helping each other, it pulled on every heart string available. When I showed the Red Cross team the first cut, there wasn't a dry eye in the house. I used the pictures and images to connect with the audience in a heartfelt, emotional way. But I used the text to fill in the details and really tell the story of what the Red Cross accomplished. There was music added to this video, but if it were never heard, the video would be just as effective.

I also use text like this to move the story along and build tension in all of my social media posts. One of the places where it is most effective are on popular social media platforms' "Stories" feature. Snapchat, Instagram, Facebook, and even LinkedIn feature these short-lived (they disappear in 24 hours) posts that attempt to give audiences a sneak peek into the lives and work of their favorite people and brands. It was originally a less-polished piece of content that provided some spur-of-the-moment or behind-the-scenes content for audiences. Now that people have figured out how to use them for marketing, they've become more polished. The novelty of having them live for such a short time, along with the neat little tools they have available, has made their engagement skyrocket. As an example, one day I did a series of Instagram Stories in 2020 about building my daughter's playset. I showed all the parts, laying on the floor, followed by a picture of me looking scared. In the next Story, I just posted text that read: "Then this happened..." followed by a picture of the final product, standing in all its sturdy gloriousness. I think that is still one of my highest performing "Stories."

People like to watch more than they like to read. Showing is more effective than telling. But sometimes, it's easy to get to your point fast by using a simple group of strong words that help tell your story effectively. Text isn't going anywhere. It is, and has been the most consistent storytelling tool since all we had was the spoken word. In 1936, Charlie Chaplin made *Modern Times*, a film that ended his run of silent films as his most famous character "The Tramp," and officially put the last nail in the coffin for the silent film era (although "talkies" had been around for nine years at that point) with the last line of the film:

"Buck up -- Never say die. We'll get along!"

EMPATHY: THE ALL-PURPOSE STORYTELLING TOOL

Any of these tools will help your ability to tell compelling stories. But you may not have access to all of them, or you may not have the skill to use them. At the end of the day, how effective you are at telling stories does not come back to your mastery of these tools. Being able to identify who your audience is, what they are going through, and what they need to overcome it, and then telling them a story that illustrates *how* to do it, is the skill that trumps all others.

It comes back to understanding your people. It comes back to having heart. It comes back to empathy. And fortunately for you, this is a tool that comes already built into your ability as a human, and you can use it to fix almost any problem your brand or business is experiencing. If you understand those core principles and values of humankind, then you will be able to use whatever tool you have access to at the moment to deliver your message and inspire people to take action. So like mastering anything, whether it be writing, or investing, or being able to do a flying push-up like a street workout athlete, you must first master the basics. And for a business owner, nonprofit director, entrepreneur, or influencer, understanding your customers, clients, and community, empathizing with their struggles, and being able to clearly convey how you can help them are the basic skills. Master them and then look for the tools to make your job easier and help you serve more people. Remember, first you have to crawl, then you can walk, then run, and then jump. And then, once you put all those skills and tools together, you can fly.

Chapter 6
THE POWER OF VIDEO STORYTELLING

When I first started my filmmaking career, the miniDV tape format was dominating the "prosumer" market and the digital revolution had completely changed the game. My predecessors had clunky, expensive film cameras, huge and hot tungsten lights that took forever to cool down, and editing suites that filled up whole rooms and cost upwards of $50,000. By the time I graduated college in 2005, I had purchased a used Sony PD170 for $2500 and was editing on a $3000 Apple Power Mac G5 that I received as a college graduation present. It was quite the gift, but I was the first person in my family to graduate college, so Mom was pretty proud. But by 2012 when I was traveling the world to make *Raise Up*, I was shooting on a Canon 60D, a DSLR camera I bought for $1200 that was smaller than my PD170, shot in much higher quality, and recorded onto reusable media (SD cards) that were 1/10th of the size of the old miniDV tapes. I was also editing on a laptop that cost $2000, but I could slide into my backpack and edit my feature length film while on a plane to Latvia. The game had changed.

If anything is as powerful as telling a person a story in person, it's using video storytelling. Dr. Zak and his team proved that. Not only that, but video now dominates about 80% of all internet traffic. You have 4k video available on your smartphone and free editing software that comes automatically installed on it.Billions of people around the world currently have the ability to make a feature length film just sitting in their pockets. This is a massive opportunity that most small to medium-sized businesses and nonprofits still haven't fully capitalized on.

All that being said, most business creatives aren't professional video creators, so there are some basics to video storytelling that we must go over. Just because you have easy access to the tools, it doesn't mean you automatically know how to use them effectively. There are some basic concepts, principles, and skills of filmmaking that you need to learn. As an independent low-budget documentary filmmaker, I learned most of these through real life work experience. My college had film and video production classes, but not a production major, so I had to learn all I could out in the field. I started working on no-budget documentaries and films when I was still in school. I initially started off acting in these films, since I had some experience acting on stage as a kid. But once production started, I'd hang around the set and ask if I could help in other ways. No one was getting paid, so the directors, sometimes pleasantly puzzled, would happily agree.

Later, I studied under a few documentary directors that were trying to resurge their careers and learned what to do when making a low-to-no budget film (as well as what not to do). After a year or two, I figured if they could bumble their way through it, I could, too. And maybe I could do it better myself. In 2006 I started my first company, Flying Flounder Productions, shooting wedding videos and sports recruiting videos for high school athletes. Each year I progressed, learning more of the basic skills and even mastering some. When I look back on some of that early footage though, it's pretty cringe-worthy. But fifteen years later, I'm still learning every time I'm on set or location.

Just like I learned as I went along, you will, too. One of the main things I want you to take away from this book is that there is no barrier to entry except the ones you have in your head. Video storytelling is an extremely powerful (and if done well, quite profitable) opportunity for you and your business. But you need to fully take advantage of it. Start where you are, with what you have, and get better and better each day. So if you're ready to go on this journey with me, there are some basic skills and knowledge you'll need to get started as well as some for when you're ready to scale.

CAMERA OPTIONS

The first thing you're going to need for video storytelling is the video part. When I was making *Raise Up*, the most common question I was asked was what camera I was using. The tech-friendly community expected me to have a much better camera than them since I was a "professional filmmaker." They expected me to have some inside scoop that they didn't have access to. In reality, many times they had much better cameras than I did. If you look on any filmmaking forum, attend any marketing or video conference, or just browse tech videos on YouTube, you'll find endless discourse and debates about what camera packages are the best. Let's discuss some of them now. And while there are certainly some camera options I'm leaving out (Cinema cameras, ENG-style cameras, etc.), those are mostly options that will be far too advanced for your level, or that will be used by a video production company like mine that you have hired out to do your video production. The camera options I discuss below are going to be the ones you, as a beginner to intermediate user, will most likely use for your video content creation. Let's get into it.

DSLR CAMERAS

By far the most popular cameras on the market are DSLR cameras—for now, at least. I say that as earnestly as possible because what used to take decades to dethrone dominant technological devices, now only takes years, and sometimes even months. DSLR stands for "digital single lens reflex." That's not really important to know if you're not a photographer, but hey... now you know. Basically, if you're seeing a camera out there that looks like a still camera, but someone is using it for video, it's probably a DSLR camera. Nikon introduced the first DSLR camera in 1999. Digital capabilities made things so much easier for photographers to take, store, and process photographs. It revolutionized photography and all other major brands soon followed suit. In 2008, Nikon decided to make some upgrades and, rumor has it, included a video feature as a special perk. No one anticipated the impact it would have. No one anticipated how good it would be! I remember seeing people using them in 2009 and 2010 and I didn't get it. I was still shooting on miniDV tape with a Sony Z1U—a fine camera, but with its fixed lens, it didn't have nearly the cinematic look the DSLRs had. It looked like a video camera. With the ability to interchange lenses,

DSLR users could buy a cheap camera body and outfit it with a great lens and the images they were creating were phenomenal. DSLRs became rapidly adopted by professionals and consumers. It revolutionized the entire industry.

I bought my first DSLR in 2013 in Madrid. It was a Canon 60D—not as professional as its brother the Canon 5D, which was even used to make feature films and TV shows at the time, but it was affordable and had a flip-out LCD screen which the 5D did not. This camera was so tiny compared to my Sony Z1U from 2007, which required its own separate bag to carry it in. The 60D could slide into my bookbag and I barely felt the difference. It was perfect for traveling the world to make a documentary. I purchased one zoom lens, a 20mm-135mm, to do the work for my "run-and-gun" style of shooting.

MIRRORLESS CAMERAS

Now, video cameras are getting even smaller with the advent of what are called "mirrorless" cameras. Mirrorless cameras look very similar to DSLRs, so most people reading this wouldn't be able to visibly tell the difference and even many people using cameras use the terms interchangeably (and incorrectly). Because mirrorless cameras don't use the mirror systems DSLRs do, the lens is much closer to the sensor, which causes them to be smaller. That's all you need to know: they're smaller, they're lighter, and they do the same quality of work. They do look a little more "plastic-y" and amateur. But again, we don't care about looks, we care about the quality of our content. Right?

Historically, mirrorless cameras didn't have interchangeable lenses and they suffered in comparison to the performance of DSLRs. They were mostly used by amateurs who had simple "point and shoot" cameras popular in the early 2000s. But now that companies like Olympus and Panasonic have focused their efforts on dominating the mirrorless market by creating a new lens mount system that allows their mirrorless cameras to interchange lenses, mirrorless cameras are becoming much more of an option for you and me, trying to create powerful and professional brand videos.

Whew, I really nerded out there for a bit. Hope you're still with me. Anyways, I currently use a Panasonic GH5. It's mirrorless.

Even though the world of photography and videography has changed drastically in the past ten years and given people like you and me the capability to produce professional quality content for much cheaper than years prior, DSLRs and mirrorless cameras still aren't necessarily considered cheap for most people. A good camera body will cost $1000 to $3000 and good lenses will cost even more! Plus, you still have to buy batteries, SD cards, camera cages to make them easier to hold and operate, gimbals, and all other kinds of accessories if you want a kit comparable to a professional's. The costs can elevate quickly.

Then, of course, you need to know how to actually use it. Sure there are countless hours of tutorials on YouTube (a resource I cannot advocate for enough), but do you have the time? Does your small but mighty team have the time? If your team at least has a marketing department, then your answer may be "yes." In that case, it may make the most sense to invest in an in-house camera package so that you can internally produce your own videos. But if your marketing team consists of one individual, like many of the organizations I've worked with, the answer will most likely be "no." So instead, your interaction with DSLRs and mirrorless cameras will probably come when you hire a filmmaker or video production company to create your marketing videos and you hear them running around speaking in technical jargon that sounds like gibberish to you. But at least now you can ask them, "Is that a DSLR or mirrorless camera?"

And they'll give you a nod of approval because you know your stuff.

ACTION CAMERAS

Another cheaper option today is what's known as an "action camera." The most recognizable brand in this market is by far the company GoPro, founded by Nick Woodman. Though the concept of action cameras, or helmet cameras, had been used for decades, Woodman's GoPro was the first small, durable, and waterproof option marketed towards average consumers. The early adopters, and still most popular users, were people with active lifestyles and hobbies. That included skydivers, mountain bikers, skiers, surfers, skaters, and the like. The size and durability of GoPros allowed them to fit in small areas and get unique angles— like the "helmet cam" or clamped to the handlebars to get the point of view from the bike—that captured the experience of the particular action like never before. It gave those people who didn't participate in the sport or activity a new perspective in which to view it. The popularity of GoPro since 2004 has skyrocketed and extended far past the active sports and lifestyle markets. For my friends in the filmmaking and video production business, it provided an easy and interesting new camera angle that could be used in production. This was a cheaper alternative to increase production value than renting another DSLR camera for a second angle.

During production for my documentary, *Finding Croatoan* (you remember the crowdfunding drone story from Chapter Two, right?), I was following a group of archaeologists who were on the brink of solving "America's Oldest Mystery," the disappearance of the "Lost Colony" of Roanoke Island—the first attempt of an English colony in the New World. Well, this all happened in what is now known as Buxton, North Carolina, near Cape Hatteras. My producing partner David and I were the only crew members (hence the need for crowdfunding) and we spent two weeks in the woods of the Outer Banks documenting the dig. The problem was, since we were out in the field, we had to have plenty of battery life for our two main cameras. It would take too long to go back to our motel and charge any batteries that died and there could be a crucial discovery that happened any second. The other problem was, there were just two of us and at least 20 people on site! We knew we wanted to show the audience how these digs actually happened, because understanding the layers of dirt in archaeology is critical to understanding the relevance to any findings and most people probably hadn't been on an archaeological dig. But David and I couldn't afford to dedicate one of our two main cameras to people digging the pit that took three days to dig. So we took our GoPro and clamped it to a tree branch, set it on a timelapse, and let it record for three days. All we had to do was periodically change the battery and replace the SD card when it was full. This gave us three days of coverage of the pit digging process, that we could then condense down to a one to two minute segment that showed the steps and team required. Furthermore, it gave the audience a unique "in the trees" perspective which made them feel like they were getting true behind-the-scenes content that they could only get in our film. The GoPro was the only kind of camera that could have done that so easily and affordably.

When considering what camera to use, or how to use them, for your brand's videos, think about the practicality of an action camera. Would that help what you're trying to capture? How could you utilize its compact frame and durable build? Could you put it on the assembly line conveyor belt to show your manufacturing company's process? Could you strap it to your customer's helmet as they fall from the sky with your skydiving instructors? Could you clamp it onto the arm rest of your salon chair as you cut a client's hair? Yes! Yes to all of these and many, many more. But beyond serving as your "B camera" to capture creative angles, an action camera is perfect to capture your vlogs, hobbies (especially if they're active ones) and personal videos. The two other ways I use mine are for family vacations—I don't have to lug around a heavy camera (it fits in my pocket) and they go shoot under water for beach vacations— and recording speeches where using a tripod is impossible or would obstruct someone's view. The ease of use and portability of action cameras provides numerous solutions to keep your content capturing from being a huge inconvenience.

The action camera option could be perfect for you for a variety of reasons: budget, durability, or its compact size. But like any decision you make, you first have to think of your end goal and the objective you're trying to accomplish first. Then, you make the decision of what tool is best.

SMARTPHONE CAMERAS

The last and undoubtedly most common camera that marketers, business owners, and entrepreneurs beginning their video storytelling journeys will have access to is the built-in camera in their smartphones. Even though the cost of a smartphone is now more comparable to a cheaper DSLR or mirrorless camera than an action camera, this is a cost that most people have already budgeted for, as their phones are much more than cameras. They are basically tiny pocket computers that also can capture video. At least that's how they started. But with the rise of social media and apps like Instagram, Snapchat, and TikTok, the demand for the video to be better has risen astronomically, and therefore the quality of the cameras have as well.

What's great about shooting video with your smartphone is that the majority of the time, that's the same device that your audience will be using to watch it. This makes the transition from production to distribution much more seamless than if you had to shoot a video on a DSLR, take the SD card out, download the footage onto your hard drive, edit it on your laptop, export it, upload it back to your phone, and then post it on Instagram. If you shoot it on your phone from the beginning, you eliminate almost all of those steps. I can't tell you how many clients don't know what to do with a bunch of video files on a hard drive. And you may not either.

Moreover, in 2021 the viewership of videos has changed to a widely mobile platform and it has created a new expectation of how videos will look. When I was starting my career, high definition (HD) footage shot in 16x9 aspect ratio (that's industry speak for widescreen format/horizontal orientation) was just starting to dominate the older standard definition (SD) 4x3 footage. I had to learn how to compose a compelling shot in a much wider frame. I remember one of my mentors teaching me how to "fill the frame" instead of just capturing the main image in the dead center of the frame and leaving the sides of the frame full of "dead space." I worked for years and finally mastered filling the frame in compelling, balanced ways. Then, when smartphones became more prevalent and people began posting their smartphone videos online, I (and probably any video production professional) would scream at the screen "Turn the camera sideways!" People would naturally shoot their video in the way they were used to holding their phones, vertically. But we professionals knew it should be horizontally. Well guess what happened? Things changed. That meant I (and all those other video production pros) had to change with it, or get left behind. Square 1x1 aspect ratio video and images, made popular by the Instagram model, started performing better than the widescreen 16x9 videos. Now, vertical video, which is 9x16 aspect ratio, made popular by Snapchat and TikTok, is dominating square.

The thing is, no matter what era, people want to consume and engage with content in the least resistant way. That means they don't want the inconvenience of having to turn their phones sideways to view the biggest version of the video they're watching. So content creators make it easier for them by shooting vertical video. That means anything from personal vlogs to Hollywood movie trailers are now edited for vertical video. If you shoot your video content on your phone, you must consider the end placement of the video while you're in production, and not find yourself realizing that the shot you composed in widescreen doesn't work when you go to make a vertical video out of it. There are apps that can reformat videos for you, but if you do it right when shooting the video, you don't have to pay or take time to fix it later.

By far the most appealing thing to beginner video storytellers about using their smartphones is simply the accessibility. They already have it and they already know how to use it. What often prevents them from using them, however, is the fear that the quality of the footage will be crap and therefore no one will take their content seriously. They think that there is some minimum production quality that must be achieved in order to make compelling videos. What I am trying to accomplish with this book is to get you to understand that it doesn't matter what tool you use, if you understand how to perfect and use the skill of storytelling. Remember, no tool is better than the hand that holds it. No one tells a master carpenter he needs to get a more expensive hammer. So no one should tell you (and it's most often your inner voice telling you) that you can't make an awesome video that creates maximum impact with your smartphone. If you understand just the fundamental basics of video production, it will open your eyes to new ways you can use your smartphone to capture and create great stories.

LIGHTING OPTIONS

Nothing makes a viewer tune out before they can tune in like not being able to clearly see the image they are looking at on the screen. Have you ever seen a couple on the beach trying to get that perfect selfie with the sunset behind them and not understanding why their faces are so dark? It's because of a thing called "backlighting." Now, have you ever seen that person who takes the beach selfie and has that golden glow of the sun making them look like a model? That's because they understood the simple concept of the main light source being on the main subject—in this case, their face!

Most lighting equipment used to be expensive, heavy, and challenging to use. I used to have to carry a 75-pound light kit all over Washington, DC while my producer (the one who taught me to "fill the frame") carried nothing. I'd arrive to set up an interview for some high level general at the Pentagon and be drenched from sweat. My 2006 self is still a bit salty. But ultimately, it's a good thing that light kits are smaller and lighter now, because that helps you. Plus, they're way cheaper, so that helps you even more. But, that doesn't mean they are any easier to understand how to use. Understanding lights and shadows and how to manipulate them is an art and science all on its own. Understanding what lights you can afford, what lights are best for the type of videos you shoot, and what type of lights would you be able to set up with ease each time you shoot is even more challenging.

The good thing is, no matter what light kit you might purchase, or how expensive and complex it is, they are all trying to replicate one light out there that's free for everyone to use: the sun. Back in the early days of cinema that we discussed in Chapter Five, motion pictures were made only using the sun. In fact, a guy that you've probably never heard of, Thomas Edison, built a studio with a retractable roof (much like AT&T Stadium, for my Dallas Cowboys fans) that sat upon a pivoting platform that would rotate the whole studio to stay aligned with the sun. It was known as the Black Maria, since it resembled a boxy police "patty wagon." The constant inventor, Edison moved away from the Black Maria in 1901 when he created a new studio with a glass roof. But ultimately, things were too unpredictable when relying on the sun in the ever-changing weather of the east coast. So the whole industry moved to a place where it never rains—Hollywood. And that's why Los Angeles became the movie capital of the world.

If you want to take your videos to the next step towards Hollywood filmmaker status, but you don't have any lights, then the first thing you need to do is figure out where the sun is. It shouldn't be that hard. The second thing you need to do is figure out how to make it work for you. That's a bit harder. The light cast from the sun should illuminate what you want people to see. So just like Edison rotated his whole stage, you need to rotate the person you are filming (even if it's you shooting selfie-style) towards the sun. However, you should be cautious that if the sun is directly in front of someone's face, it can be too bright and actually wash them out making their face look flat. The secondary purpose of lighting someone (besides just making them visible to the audience) is to show that they are three dimensional. You achieve this by having your primary light, known as a "key light", strike them at an angle (45 degrees or so) instead of head on. This creates shadows on their face and shows the audience they are real people with real faces. To achieve this, just get the person on camera to turn their body slightly. They'll also appreciate it, because now they won't be blinded by the light ("revved up like a deuce, another runner in the night!" Sorry, I couldn't help it.)

When I was preparing to travel to Europe in 2013 for *Raise Up*, I had to be very careful about what I decided to bring, since I only had two bags. Fortunately, I was broke and couldn't afford much equipment, so this problem kind of solved itself. But after my trip to Latvia the previous year for the Street Workout World Championship, I learned that if I was going to make a real documentary (regardless of the lack of budget), I needed to have some sort of lighting with me. But there was no way I could carry a whole light kit around the world for six months and I certainly didn't have the money to buy or rent one. During the month before I left, I was living at my brother's house in North Carolina. I did some freelance work for my producer friend John. We were shooting a food cookoff (think "Iron Chef") that Food Lion created to showcase an affordable healthy food campaign they were promoting. We were in the tight quarters of a small kitchen but needed to show the fine details like the amateur chefs chopping herbs or fileting a fish. So John's solution was to use these small LED lights that were mounted on our DSLR cameras. They were only about five inches wide but produced a ton of light. I knew this would be the perfect solution for making my film when all I could bring were two bags for my equipment and clothing for six months. What made them even more perfect for my situation, was that they were only $100—a small investment for what might've possibly saved my film from the fate of almost all other low-budget documentaries.

A lot of the time, most of the street workout competitions I was filming were outside, so I could also use the sun. If I was interviewing a top athlete, I would use the sun as my key light. The LED panel came in super handy to serve as my "fill light." The fill light is the secondary light source whose job is to fill in some of the shadows that the key light created. Often, if the key light is very bright (like, say, this sun we keep talking about), the shadows it creates across someone's face can be harsh and distracting. The fill light comes in to even that out a little bit. Having this little light allowed me to get great looking interviews that only took five minutes to set up. When we weren't outside at the competitions, I'd be following the behind-the-scenes culture of this movement and that meant capturing conversations and antics in the hotels and partying in the clubs after the competitions. In these cases, the LED panel was my only light, therefore becoming my key light, and was a complete lifesaver for some moments I caught that otherwise would have been hard to watch.

If you are at the point where your business is spending more time creating video stories, this is my first suggestion for your lighting solutions. Invest a little bit of money to give you a portable light you can control. It will save you more times than you can count, you'll get your money's worth in one shoot, and it'll have your videos much closer to professional filmmaker status. Currently, with the dramatic increase in influencers and "solopreneurs" creating video content, a lighting option called a "ring light" has appeared on the consumer market. Shaped like a circle and originally made for taking dental photographs of teeth, ring lights quickly became popular for makeup and fashion models, as they easily illuminated the entire face in a balanced way. Now, they are used by all kinds of creators because they are cheap, usually plug into a USB port, and still very small. Some are larger and require a tripod, but many are super small and portable just like the on-camera LED light I used for *Raise Up*.

However, if your business gets to the point where you are consistently producing high-quality video content—examples could be weekly live videos, "how to" YouTube videos, online video courses, or even short documentaries like we do at Six Second Stories—you're going to want to ante up and invest in a decent light kit. Fortunately for you, it doesn't have to be the 75lb Arri kit I carried around DC the summer of 2006. In fact, what I use currently might be perfect for your situation and budget. Each month, I travel once or twice to conduct video interviews for documentaries I produce for the Neuroendocrine Cancer Foundation. You may remember me mentioning this client in Chapter Four. I travel solo for these shoots to manage costs and efficiency. But taking a page out of my *Raise Up* book, I knew that I didn't want to lug hard, heavy cases through multiple airports when I'd sometimes be on four flights in one day. So I bought a light kit that can break down and fit into my checked luggage. I have two flat 1ft x 1ft LED panels that produce a great amount of light and adjustable color temperature (for a warmer or cooler feel), three light stands, my tripod, and my trusty little on-camera LED light (that now has some cracks and scars, but it's traveled around the world so it's much wiser and cultured).

The small LED light has been demoted and now serves as my "back light," or the third point of the "three point lighting" technique. As you remember from above, the key light is the main source of light to create depth and dimension and the fill light fills in those shadows for a more evenly lit image. The back light (which goes behind the subject), outlines the person's body you're filming and separates them from the background. You can obviously use so many more lights and equipment to diffuse or direct the lights, but if you understand this basic knowledge of three point lighting, you will be able to create amazing looking videos without a lot of expensive equipment. This is the simplest way to achieve a professional looking interview and it can all break down and fit into a suitcase, and cost me less than $300. (Luggage fees are not included in that price, unless I fly Southwest.)

Just remember the purpose of your lights. At the end of the day, you are trying to help people see you, or the people featured in your videos. Don't overthink it. Whether recording a live video on your smartphone for social media, delivering a presentation over video conference, or producing high level short documentaries, the same concept applies: light what you want the audience's eyes to focus on the most.

AUDIO OPTIONS

You learned back in Chapter Five how important great audio is— perhaps even more important than great video, right? But when you're lacking equipment, or the funds to get good equipment, or the time to even set up good equipment if you actually had the funds to purchase it, how can you still secure the level of audio quality you need to not look completely amateurish? In the real estate world, the three most important things to consider when buying property are "location, location, location." In the audio world, it's the same thing. When you want to secure good audio, you have to consider three very specific locations.

The first and most important of the three "locations" is the location you are recording. It simply needs to be as quiet a location as possible. If you're in the middle of a busy conference, and you only have this one chance to secure a testimonial from a very important person who will endorse your business, you'll want to see if you can get them out of that busy room and tucked away somewhere quiet. A hallway is a decent option, but a private room is even better. When I'm shooting documentary footage at a hospital and securing a room to conduct an interview, I specifically request a conference room (not the doctor's office) and preferably not one in a high-traffic area of the building. You must always consider this before you start shooting. Will you be outside? Because outdoors will always have uncontrollable audio variables like airplanes overhead, dogs barking, and construction. Or if you're in that busy conference mentioned above, will there be a PA system or loudspeaker that could overtake your subject speaking at any time? Before your start, always look around your location, and listen.

The second most important "location" of the three is the smaller details of the location you secure. When I book that conference room in the hospital, I prefer to be able to check it out beforehand, but often that is not the case. So, many times I have issues that I have to troubleshoot just before the interview starts.

The three problems I most often face, in order of frequency, are HVAC/electronics noise, bad echo, and leaf blowers! The heating system, especially in large institutions like hospitals and schools, are not always adjustable for individual rooms, but rather run on a building-wide system. That means I can't just change the thermostat and wait for the system to shut off for my interview. Large scale heating systems are often loud and this can create a lot of unnecessary background noise. It sucks. But it's a part of what I have to deal with and you may, too. Sometimes you get lucky, and you find a big room in an area of the building where no one goes and it looks cool because it has floor-to-ceiling glass windows and OMG it's perfect! Except when you listen back to your audio and it's completely echoey because there's not a shred of carpet in the room to dampen the sound. (Eventually you'll get better at noticing this beforehand, but most novices completely overlook this issue, which is why you'll need to train your ear.) And lastly, the dreaded leaf blower. Leaf blowers are the gods' cruelest version of Murphy's Law ever. They are inevitable. Imagine you've found the right room, which looks stunning, sounds great and there's no foot traffic or people yammering in the background, and you have space to set up your equipment and carve out a nice depth of field in your shot composition. Then just as you hit Record, you hear, "weeeeeeeeeeeeeeeeee!" and your heart stops. The maintenance crew chose this day, and even this hour to run their leafblowers, weed-eaters, floor buffers, jack-hammers and any and all other noise-makers known to man. These are the struggles that crush souls.

But all of these issues that may arise in the first and second locations can likely be combated by the third location—the location of your microphone. To put it as simply as I can put it (and I'm stealing these words directly from my audio mixer who's shouted

them at me at least 47 times): MOVE THE MICROPHONE CLOS-
ER! How many times have you been at an event and someone
who's not used to, or not comfortable, speaking into a microphone starts to let their hand holding the microphone drift down
towards their chest until some A/V tech mime-yells, "Hold the
mic closer to your mouth!" Everyone in the audience hasn't heard
a word the speaker has said since the mic passed his or her chin.
This is the same issue you will face. If the mic is too far away from
your speaker's mouth, especially if you are facing competing noise
issues, your audience won't be able to hear them, no matter how
good your equipment is.

But if you know that basic rule first, the equipment that you
use will have a huge impact on the quality of audio you can capture, regardless of the noise factors and locations you face. If you
have no audio equipment, I cannot plead with you enough to get
something! If you don't, you'll be forced to use the in-camera microphones which are equally terrible whether you have a $15,000
cinema camera or your $1000 smartphone. Nevertheless, you'll
sometimes find yourself in a situation where you don't have anything else (but you need to capture that video testimonial from
your VIP). So if that's the case, follow the location rules above
as strictly as you can. But if you do have the time and budget to
get some audio equipment for your video productions, there are
three solid options you should explore.

*A brief note about microphone pickup patterns before the next
part: there are four main pickup patterns you should know at least
at a base level. There are more, but you just need the basics here.
Omnidirectional mics pickup sound in every direction—these are
usually harder to isolate individual sounds. Bidirectional mics
pickup sound in front of the mic and behind it—these are common-*

ly used in radio or podcasts, where there are two speakers facing one another. Directional mics pickup sound directly in front of them—these are typically used in documentary or scripted video productions. Cardioid mics pickup sound in a heart-shaped pattern, meaning everything but what's directly behind the mic—these are used commonly in music or live performances to make sure to capture all sounds in front of the mic.

SHOTGUN MIC

Despite the name, this microphone is completely safe to use and only runs the risk of blowing away your past mistakes capturing audio. Wow, that joke was terrible. We're leaving it in, though. You probably already have heard of this type of microphone. You may have even mistakenly called it a "boom mic," which could be acceptable if it were on a boom pole at the time. But if it's attached to your camera, it's just a "shotgun mic." It actually looks more like a handgun to me. Either way, it is similar to a gun in that it shoots at whatever you point it at. A shotgun mic typically has a directional pattern, which means if you drew a straight line out from the tip of the mic, it would pick up whatever was right in front of it. That means: point it at the mouth of your subject! If you turn it slightly, you'll see a big difference. Sometimes shotgun mics use a cardioid pattern, though. A cardioid pattern is similar to directional in that it captures what's in front of the mic, but it captures *everything* in front of the mic and not just the specific area directly in front of it. It's more versatile and an audio person might prefer this if they are picking up two people having a conversation, for example, because it would capture both of their voices well. What makes the shotgun mic option so great is that it really reduces background sound (anything the mic is not pointing at). It doesn't eliminate it by any means, but it makes those testimonials in the corner of a busy conference a little easier to hear. These range anywhere from $50 to $350 and can attach to most any camera you'll be using to tell your video stories. Yes, that even means your smartphone or tablet! Huge win.

LAVALIER MIC

A lavalier microphone has sometimes been referred to as a "lapel mic" because it's the little mic that is usually pinned on someone's (often a news anchor or TV personality) lapel, collar, or tie. These microphones are often omnidirectional so that if someone turns their head, it won't drastically affect the quality of the audio being captured. Also, since the mic is usually very close to the person's voice box, being omnidirectional doesn't create as many issues as it would if you used an omnidirectional mic for capturing an event, with a lot of competing sounds. There are a few main reasons you would want to use this microphone. First, if you don't have room in your shot for a person to get close enough with a shotgun microphone without seeing it in the video frame (pro tip: you do *not* want that), a lavalier mic is a perfect (and sneaky!) way to get a mic close to the subject's mouth. Secondly, it allows you to grab good quality audio even if you are far away from a person (like a groom at a wedding, when the camera needs to be far away from the altar—or someone giving a safety demonstration where the camera needs to be away from any danger—or just with a subject who is moving around a lot). Wireless lavalier mics changed the game for situations like this since they aren't tethered to audio recorder/receiver, and are the preferred way to go—although I can hear Mike, my audio guy, saying "wired mics are much more reliable!" in my head right now. Lastly, many people use lavaliers as a second option for recorded audio. A backup is always a good idea. Opinion is divided as to whether the shotgun mic should serve as the primary mic and the lavalier as the backup, or vice versa. I've heard it both ways. But, from my experience, most professional audio engineers prefer the audio from a shotgun mic than a lavalier mic, and most amateurs prefer to use the lavalier mic because they often don't have access to a larger crew (which would include an audio engineer to operate and monitor the shotgun mic). Just know that a good set can be expensive—from $500 to $1000. But like almost all the equipment we've discussed in this chapter, cheaper and easier-to-use options that play to the smartphone crowd are hitting the market every day. Either way, this little guy can be a crucial member in your audio arsenal.

PORTABLE AUDIO RECORDER

Another option for recording sound in the "field" or on location is what's known as a portable audio recorder, or "handy" recorder. If you're not my audio guy, Mike, and you don't want to be carrying around a full sized heavy audio mixing board strapped to your body, this is a great option to record multiple tracks of audio. The best part about these, besides the portability, is the versatility. These audio recorders typically come with a good quality microphone already built in the device itself. But then they also allow professional audio cable inputs called XLR (these will be the cables used from any professional sound recording device, like if you wanted to get a copy of the audio from the soundboard at a concert), as well as the more consumer standard 1/8 inch audio cable inputs (this is what's most commonly referred to as an auxiliary or "aux" cable that goes in a headphone jack).

There are many brands offering versions of this device, but Zoom and Tascam are probably the most popular. The most common ways I use my Zoom H4N (which is ancient now but still does the job well!) is for recording podcasts on the go (if I can't bring my full setup), recording something from far away if I can't get a lavalier on the person or just want ambient background sound, recording an audio feed from the soundboard of one of my speeches, and to record the audio from the lavalier mic in an interview I'm conducting (my DSLR camera doesn't have an XLR cable input, so I have to record the audio separately and sync it later, and I use a small camera-mounted shotgun mic as a backup).

All of these audio options have their place and function and you have to consider your unique situation to know which one will serve you best. But if I can leave you with my most valuable audio advice that I've learned, it's: 1) test and monitor your audio by wearing headphones 2) always use a backup microphone and 3) get the microphone as close as possible!

A FINAL EQUIPMENT OVERVIEW

You know that my goal is to make you a compelling storyteller first, and then a technical video creator second. But the fact remains that the more educated you are about the field, and the tools used in the field, the better you will be able to complete the task of creating powerful video content that inspires change in your audience. Yes, you have all the tools you need to start right now. But the only way you can continue to get better is to keep adding tools to your toolbox.

The main thing I need you to know is that while storytelling in any format is effective, and you should utilize it, video is by far going to be your strongest weapon moving forward in the 21st Century. I know I've told you that telling a story in person is the most effective way to tell a story, with video being a strong second option. But the difference is, unless you become a professional speaker or storyteller like me, you will most likely only be able to use live storytelling in a one-to-one or one-to-a-few basis. You will never be able to compete with video's ability to reach hundreds, thousands, and even millions of people. This is why it is your most powerful weapon. If you can tell great stories, your messages will stick in the minds of your audience. But if you use video to tell those stories, they can spread across the globe to other people you could help faster than Superman trying to reverse time to save the life of Lois Lane. (No, I *will not stop using movie examples from the 1970s.*)

PART THREE

MAXIMIZE YOUR IMPACT IN MINIMAL TIME

3

Chapter 7
SHORT FORM VIDEO

There is a question that has existed since the beginning of time about storytelling—one that may haunt us just as much as how many licks it takes to get to the center of a Tootsie Roll Pop.

It has plagued marketers, writers, artists, and entrepreneurs for years. That question is: "How long should a story be?" And the answer is that perpetually frustrating phrase, "it depends." Or like many of my storytelling expert friends might say (even more frustratingly to their audiences), "A story should be as long as it should be." What does that even mean?! Well my go-to answer might just be the best attempt at solving this riddle of all time. But I can't take credit for it. The credit goes to my college Creative Writing professor, a proud Scot. He told our class that "a story should be like a man's kilt—long enough to cover the subject, but short enough to remain interesting." That might take you a second, but you'll get it. And it's perfect.

EDITING YOUR VIDEOS TO THE RIGHT LENGTH

The same thing applies to your videos. There are no "rules" except those of your distribution channel. However, there does seem to be an unwritten rule in this time of smartphones and social media: the shorter, the better. I'm not sure that's necessarily true, but I would be negligent to not recognize that our attention spans seem to be getting shorter and the list of things demanding that attention seems to be getting longer. In almost every speech I hear about marketing, someone brings up the overused and debatable statistic that "our attention spans are shorter than those of goldfish (8.2 seconds)" in their slideshow. They say things like, "You must get your message across in as short of a time as possible and hook your audience in the first two seconds any way possible!" I get the point and it is one worth commenting on, but I strongly believe that if you tell a great story, you don't have to use gimmicks to grab their attention. What I want you to focus on in terms of brevity are the things great storytellers have always focused on: how to move the story forward, creating and releasing tension, as efficiently as possible.

I see people in my workshops stressed about this. It's one of the most asked questions that I get. But it's not just that a video should be short for the sake of being short because people don't have long attention spans. Comedian Bill Burr explained it best when talking about crafting and editing down a joke. "You have to get a joke down to where if you took just one more word out, the joke wouldn't work." That means you *only* keep in the information most essential to the joke and cut everything else. And storytelling is the exact same. That doesn't mean that there's no room for colorful language or even peripheral details. It just means that all of the information included must have a purpose. The goal of any story is to keep it engaging and move it forward.

The reality of our current state of media consumption, however, does place us in a position where we are competing with more content than ever before to get the attention of our audiences. As television producer and author Brant Pinvidic says in this book on the art of pitching, *The 3-Minute Rule*, "It's not that we're all dumbed-down, mindless, distracted zombies—it's actually just the opposite. In fact, people today focus more *intensely* and *efficiently*. The proliferation of technology and the ability to get unlimited information instantly have created hyper-savvy consumers. They have zero tolerance for long-winded explanations, exhaustive chatter, or linguistic sales tactics. They will tune you out in an 8.2-second instant."[18]

I agree with Brant. It's *not* just that people don't have long attention spans. It's that they don't have the time or patience to dedicate that priceless attention to something that isn't important to them or their objectives. People are busier than ever before and constantly on the go. To help in our fast-paced efforts, we've developed little computers in our pockets that used to only make phone calls, but now do so much more than that, that the initial function is often overlooked. We order our food on it, we do our banking, we search for our houses, we update our websites, we message our friends, family, and colleagues, and we watch our video content. No one has the time or patience to watch a full length movie on their smartphones (unless they're on a plane) because everyone has a thousand other things to do. Only the essential stuff matters, just like in storytelling. So if you want your content to be one of the essential pieces of content for them, you've got to find the way you best fit into *their* story, and you better show them quickly.

That is why the demand for short form video has grown so much recently. Smartphones are mobile. They are meant to be used on the go. And that's where the eyes are. So you must adapt and adjust. For many people and brands, it's a struggle to figure out how to creatively fit their information into the small window that short form video allows. Exactly what "short form video" is, however, is hard to define. You'll hear a myriad of different answers. Google determines a short form video is anything shorter than 10 minutes and anything longer is considered long form. So for the purposes of this book, I'm going to stick to Google's definition as every other article I read attempting to define "short form video" was just one individual's opinion.

But beyond everybody being on the go, or most likely *because* of it, you also have to recognize that there has been a shift in the structure and boundaries of our media channels. Many distribution platforms require videos of less than 60 seconds and sometimes even 15 seconds. And if they don't require the videos to be that short, the algorithms promote videos watched in their entirety, so 15 second videos or shorter perform much better in terms of views. That means if you don't connect with your audience in that amount of time and get your messages across, you have a problem. The good thing is, now that you are well on your way to becoming a compelling storyteller, you already have the tools to fix this problem. The same rules apply when telling short form stories as they do with any length stories. You still must move the story forward, creating and releasing tension, as efficiently as possible. There are a few easy ways you can do that in the editing process with any video you create.

CUT THE FAT

We've already established that your goal with any story is to keep it moving forward. Inevitably on your first pass, you will include more information that you think is important or you like for personal reasons, anecdotes that you think are relevant or funny, or extraneous details that you think add to our story, when they really just confuse people. Then, as any compelling storyteller should do, after you work through it a few times, you should cut the fat so that you are left with only the essential content.

In the filmmaking world, the story is written three times—once during the script writing process, the second time on set when the film is in production, and the third time when it is being cut in the editing room. When any director is on set, they will inevitably find certain scenes just don't work as well as the writer had hoped when they put them on the page. Some of that has to be cut, or rearranged and shot differently than originally written. The writer may be slightly (or more than slightly) offended, but it is done to move the story forward and keep the audience engaged. Something wasn't working to accomplish those two things. But even the director isn't omnipotent. Because when the film gets in the hands of the editor, new scenes that don't work will be exposed. Either they don't feel as good or make as much sense as they did on set or, you guessed it, they don't move the story forward or keep the audience engaged. Even if it's a beautifully shot and acted scene, sometimes it has to be cut from the story. And it's a difficult process, especially when the director has fallen in love with that particular scene for a personal reason. But as Faulkner's old expression goes, they must learn to "kill their darlings" and make the best decision for the audience and the story. That exact issue is why there is such a thing as "Director's Cuts" of movies.

When I was in college in the early 2000s, I had a DVD collection that would rival anyone's. Friends would come over to my house to comb through the catalog like it was their own private Blockbuster video store (and if you don't remember those, think "Netflix," but in the form of a huge chain of brick and mortar stores). As the go-to DVD connoisseur, I always wanted to find the special edition director's cuts with all the bonus material. (The best part about DVDs that streaming video will never have is the bonus material. Thankfully, we have YouTube for all our behind-the-scenes needs.) But inevitably, when my friends and I would watch the director's cut versions, the film experience just wasn't the same as it was when we watched the theatrically released version. It was always about 20 minutes too long and didn't really add much to the experience. That's exactly why those 20 minutes were cut in the first place! No matter how cool the shot looked or how great the performance was, it didn't move the story forward or engage the audience. Guess what? As a storyteller, you are a director, too! That's right, Spielberg. You're the director of your content. So you, too, must kill your darlings and ruthlessly cut the fat. The best way to do this is to get objective feedback from others you trust before you ship out your content.

When I was making *Raise Up*, the first cut was almost three hours long. Can you believe that? Trust me, no one but my internal team saw that cut. Later that year, I had to screen a two-hour version for the athletes and attendees of the 2014 Street Workout Superfinal in Oslo (note: this was actually two and a half years *before* the official release of the movie). This wasn't exactly what you'd call a subjective audience—they were cheering because they saw themselves and their friends on the big screen—but it did give me the chance to sit back and watch the movie as a viewer instead of the creator. I saw what parts people laughed at (and whether they were supposed to laugh at that part). I saw what parts of the movie made people rustle in their seats. And I felt the last 20 minutes drag on myself! This was valuable feedback and when I got back to the States, I went to work to tell this story as efficiently as possible. Over the next two years, I screened it for audiences at fitness expositions, film festivals, and focus groups with people who knew nothing about the movie. Each and every time, I came back with at least one or two notes of what could be cut or re-edited to make the film better. Of course there were many notes that wouldn't have necessarily made it better, but when I would hear the same note several times, I knew the audience was missing something in my movie and that was a great opportunity for me to listen and learn from them—the people I was ultimately trying to impact.

By far the best feedback I received was from people close to me, who knew my goals and vision, that could still offer objective feedback. This is a skill all on its own, by the way. Most people you know just want to tell you "It's really good!" just because they're proud that you even made anything. But that's not helpful. To improve your work, you need to find those friends, colleagues, or family members that can keep it real. Along the journey of making the film, I befriended Michael, a *Men's Health* writer who was assigned to tell the story of the burgeoning sport of "street workout." I helped introduce him to the right people with the best stories and he and I became close friends. But this was a man who, 1) understood the overall story I was trying to capture and tell, and 2) was a professional writer who wouldn't BS me about the structure and what was working and not working. The best piece of advice he gave me was to eliminate all the "inside baseball" that was in my movie. I had never heard that term before, except on the actual baseball field, but I understood immediately. There were too many nuances and small details or extra characters that only those athletes in Oslo would've cared about. That's because they'd watch *anything* about this sport they loved. But if I wanted to win over the film festival crowds, or a mainstream audience, or even the focus group folks that seem to just be mad at life anyway, I had to find a way to make my story clearer. And that meant I had to get to cutting the fat and anything that didn't engage the audience and move the story forward.

Cutting the fat is not easy to do because it's hard to know where to start. When you have three main points to make and you're trying to jam them into a 15-second social media ad, it's just not going to happen. Three points to make in a 30-second spot would be hard. But when you're so close to your work, it's very hard to see what is most important and what content is just kind of important. That's why it's so crucial for you to recruit a pre-audience to view your work. Even then, you have to know that everyone has an opinion and just because they tell you something is good or bad doesn't mean it necessarily is. But if everyone is telling you the same thing, you should definitely listen. Just remember that your goal is to serve your audience. So get out of your own head and think about what they would connect to in your story and not just the story you want to tell. Once you identify those things, cut the rest. Because it's just the fat around the meat.

REMOVE REDUNDANCIES

Another problem that storytellers often have when trying to tell their stories in minimal time is a little harder to recognize than "inside baseball." More often than not, in your everyday speech as well as the stories you tell, you probably tend to be redundant. You essentially say the same things over and over and over again (see how unnecessary that was?). If you're speaking to another person, this could likely be because you are excited or passionate about the point you're trying to make. So it comes from a good place. But it causes a bad problem.

My family has a problem of telling the same story multiple times in a row. My mom does it, my brother does it, and I do it. We will finish a story and immediately repeat it word-for-word. When we're together, we don't mind it because the second time we still get a laugh, a pat on the back, a sigh, a tear, or whatever emotional response we needed to receive from it. But when I first started dating my wife, it didn't work out the same way. One day, after we had been dating a few months, she abruptly stopped me as I started my second round of the story. "Yeah, babe. You just told me this." I didn't know how to respond. I just stopped talking and stared at her. "I'm sorry, you just always do this." she said. "And I always think there's going to be some new information, but you just tell the same exact story twice!" I still had no retort. She was right. There was no new information to present, I was just wasting her time. Now if my wife sounds like the "bad guy" in this scenario, let me just clarify: she has to endure this with my mom, my brother, *and* me. I was the only one she could actually say it to, so she's still taking a few bullets for the team.

But when some marketers craft a script for a video or edit together soundbites from different interviews, they tend to do the same thing, just for a slightly different reason. It is also usually to illustrate a point they are passionate about, but more so because they think they need to emphasize it multiple times so the audience "gets it." It's either the overall message they want the audience to take away or at least something that they think is important to hear. Even though they are indeed thinking about what the audience needs to hear, it's not from a place of empathy. It's what *they* want the audience to hear, not necessarily what the audience needs or wants to hear. And because of that, insecurities can flare up and cause some marketers to repeat the same thing multiple times—which is not the way you want to reinforce the point. It's a way to lose your audience because you're wasting their time with no new information. Just like I waste my wife's time with my second stories! I made this mistake when I was writing my first narrative short film and one of my mentors said something to me that has stuck with me since. After seeing me trying too hard to reinforce the message or theme of the film, he said, "You don't need to beat them over the head with this point. Give your audience the benefit of the doubt that they can put two and two together and pick up what you're putting down."

I had a client that struggled a lot with this. This particular organization treated and housed some of the most emotionally disturbed children in their area. These were kids that had dealt with the kind of trauma you wouldn't wish on your worst enemy. The organization wanted to create a video to convey that they were doing great work, in hopes to raise money at their annual fundraiser. After our first draft, something wasn't hitting. It was way too long, for starters, and you already know that's a quick way to lose your audience. But my team had followed their initial outline and included all the points the client deemed "VERY IMPORTANT." I gave them the opportunity to tell me what we could cut in their first round of revisions but they only found a sentence or two that they thought we could remove—bringing a nine minute video down to eight minutes. We had a five minute time slot at the fundraising event and our deadline was approaching fast. I scheduled a video conference call so we could work the video line by line.

Before the call, I sent the client (there was an Operations Manager, the COO, the CEO, and an assistant going to be on the line) a document of the video's voiceover transcribed. This was an exercise I used when I desperately needed to cut down *Raise Up* after that two-hour screening in Oslo. With documentaries, I tend to have an outline, but not a written out script. Some documentaries use scripts for the entire movie, especially if they have a narrator (think Ken Burns-style historical documentaries). But I like to make documentaries that build the story through authentic interviews. Imagine writing a paragraph out of pre-written sentences. There's an art-form to it. But you sacrifice the control you have when you're operating off of a script. So one way to eliminate redundancies is to still treat it just like it is a script. Write or type it out, print it, and read it. As you read through it, you will quickly start to notice when lines don't really make sense or don't go together. But the real work is done when you go through, line by line, and write down what the line is *really* saying. I'm not talking about the words on the page, but what the core message is—what the reader or listener takes away from it. I call this process "Jerry Maguiring." Let me explain.

First of all, if you haven't seen Cameron Crowe's 1996 hit, *Jerry Maguire* (and that's totally likely now that it's 25 years old, ugh), stop what you're doing and go watch it. But if you don't have time for that, you still might recognize a couple of its famous lines. In the climax of the story Dorothy (played by Renee Zellweger) delivers one of those famous lines, "You had me at hello." But just before that, Jerry (played by Tom Cruise) is confessing his true feelings for her. They were in the middle of a "nice long break" that almost certainly was going to precede their divorce. Jerry was away on a solo work trip. But Jerry comes home abruptly. He walks back into their house on a mission and finds a living room full of women—organized by Dorothy's sister as a book club/men-hating support group. Jerry says, "Hello." and the buzzing room stops. Dorothy emerges from the kitchen and sees him. Their small sports agency had just had a very big night as their star client had an amazing performance on national TV during a contract year. But Jerry tells her it wasn't "even close to being in the same vicinity as complete, because I couldn't share it with you. I couldn't hear your voice or laugh about it with you. I miss... I missed my wife... I love you. You complete me. And not just..." She cuts him off. "Shut up. Just shut up... you had me at 'hello.'" And the rest is cinema history.

But she cut him off because he was just being redundant! If you break down each of his lines to their core message, all he is really saying is with each one is "I love you," which is something he had always struggled to admit to her, and himself. That's all she needed to hear and she didn't care about the rest. He was just wasting her time and needed to cut to the chase and kiss her!

So I use this approach whenever a client is getting long-winded or redundant in their video stories. After we "Jerry Maguired" the script for the client that dealt with emotionally traumatized children, I noticed several areas where we could cut down. There was one segment that read like this: (*first speaker, the director*) "The thing that makes us different is our staff. Day in and day out they show up and do this hard work because they love it. (*second speaker, administrator*) Our staff has been handpicked because of their passion and their experience and there is no better team suited to serve our students. (*third speaker, a staff member*) I live for this work. There is no other place I could see myself and even though it is challenging at times, the reward of seeing these stu-

148

dents excel is far worth it. (*fourth speaker, a parent*) They are just really great at what they do and I'm so glad my child is here."

When we broke down those four statements to their core messaging, they all were essentially saying the same thing! "Our staff is great and they care about this work." Granted, that message isn't colorful or even powerful, but that's the heart of the message and it needs to be conveyed. But it only needs to be said once. So we chose which one: 1) conveyed that sentiment the most, 2) sounded the strongest, and 3) came from the best perspective. The first statement got cut fast because it was from the executive director. Of course she's going to say her team is great. Also it just didn't say much. The second statement said a bit more—that they were hand selected for this team and job—and is overall a decent choice. The fourth statement could have been great since it was from a parent who ostensibly experienced working with the staff, but it wasn't very strong. The third statement was the winner. It comes from the source (the staff member themselves), their commitment is clearly shown, (what the other statements were also trying to convey) and, most of all, it had heart, which none of the others had. Remember, "show, not tell," right? Because of those reasons, the other three were cut, we reduced the running time of that segment by 75%, and we didn't lose any of the impact or sentiment. Then we just repeated the process for the rest of the segments of our film and finally reached our five minute mark.

This exercise has helped me produce tighter stories for my clients time and time again. In this environment where your audience is constantly on the go, you don't have much time to get through to them. Nothing is more insulting and boring to your audience than hearing the same thing over and over and over again (did it get you again?). To perfect this in your own videos, use the same process. If you write a script first, which often you should, make sure to read it through multiple times (and have others read it) to look for redundancies. And if you go the documentary-style route and shoot a bunch of interviews, then build your story later, take your first draft through the Jerry Maguiring process I just showed you. Take a piece of paper, draw a vertical line down the middle, write down each spoken line in the left column and then it's real meaning in the right column. When you see multiple lines in the right column that say essentially the same things, cut them!

Clarity is your goal, not repetition. Be clear the first time and you don't have to be redundant.

GET TO THE POINT FAST

Through the Jerry Maguiring method of removing redundancies, you learned how to make your point with clarity. Now you need to learn how to get there quickly. In feature films, which range anywhere from an hour to three and a half hours, we've gotten used to opening scenes that serve as an introduction to the characters we are going to follow and the worlds they inhabit. Sometimes they are slow, sometimes they are fast, but they always set you up for the story you are about to hear or watch. You see the hero or main character in their normal world, before the external conflict arises through the inciting incident that will launch our story forward. Remember all that from Chapter Three? But the practical purpose behind these introductions has been to allow the filmmakers, production companies, and studios time to display their opening credits, which can last several minutes depending on how many people negotiated to get their names on the screen. The funny thing is, this sequence has shortened dramatically since the early days of motion pictures, even though so many more people work on them now.

Historically when society transitions from one medium to another, the successor tends to emulate the predecessor (for that's all they've known) in several ways for some time, until people realize the true capabilities of the new medium and what makes the most sense for that format specifically. Remember Chapter Five when you learned the brief history of the media? The first smartphone video was shot as if it would be broadcast on televisions or desktops computers, but is now being optimized for mobile viewing. When televisions came out, they copied all the rules and formats of the motion picture industry. When motion pictures rose to popularity, all they had to base their approach on was theater.

Before any theatrical performance, playbills were posted and programs were handed out to the attendees which credited the cast and crew. People sat down and skimmed through the program to see who was involved in the production. Then, there was an intermission half way through and the curtain call after the play or musical was done. Similarly, when motion pictures rose to popularity in the early 1900s, they had title cards that displayed the cast and crew in the opening credits, the dialogue between characters in the movie, an intermission if there was one, and at the end usually just the two words: "The End." The borders of the title cards were even usually designed to look like theater curtains! As motion pictures evolved and silent films became "talkies," there was no need for the title cards reflecting what the characters were saying. We didn't need the "Intermission" or "The end" cards and we certainly didn't need to have borders on the frame that looked like theater curtains. But film producers still kept the long opening credits that often still looked like a program the audience would hold in their hands, since there were so many different names that the production company had to squeeze in there. Even though this was the most efficient way to get through the credits, it took forrrrrrever and was an absolute bore-fest.

Would you believe me if I told you that this practice stayed in effect until the late 1970s? Although shifting the full credits to the end of the film had been done a few times before, the trend didn't catch on until George Lucas's *Star Wars* in 1977, which started with its iconic text crawl and moved all the credits to after the final shot. (How apropos of a book on storytelling, with *Star Wars* being one of the most on-the-nose examples of Joseph Campbell's monomyth, "The Hero's Journey.") Since then, almost every movie has moved the majority of their credits to the end, with just key performers and players (such as the main cast, writer, director, production company, and studio) represented at the beginning. This eliminated the need for long, drawn out introductions to the films and gave us the opportunity to jump straight into the action. Which then proposed the question of whether we actually even needed an intro. When you skip the intro to your protagonist, or the world in which he or she exists, and jump straight into the story as it is happening, mid-scene, that is a method called "in medias res." *In medias res* is a Latin expression, meaning "in the midst of things." This launches the audience into the middle of the story and forces them to lock in fast, instead of gradually working their way into it. It can be quite effective.

Each summer, I write and direct a narrative short film and there is no place that this tool is more needed than a short film. And this is probably the length of time where a good portion of your video content might fall. If your total story is somewhere from one to thirty minutes, you don't have time for a long intro. You don't need to see your character waking up, showering, brushing his teeth, putting his books in his bag, heading out the door, hopping on the bus, getting off the bus, and entering the school, when the first action doesn't start until he's in the classroom. Just start with him in the classroom! The audience will put together the rest of the stuff in their head—everyone knows what it takes to get up and get ready for school! But if your character gets in a fight on the bus and your story is about him learning how to stand up for himself, then start with your character sitting on the bus. Again, your audience knows what it took for him to get there, they don't need to see it!

Not so coincidentally, *Star Wars* mastered this, as well. After the last words of the iconic text crawl disappear into space, the camera tilts down to reveal a small spaceship (the Rebel blockade runner, Tantive IV, for all my nerds out there) fleeing from the attack of a gigantic Imperial Star Destroyer, seemingly as large as the sandy planet it's flying over (that's Tatooine, ya nerds!). Boom. We've landed in the midst of a battle and are immediately sucked into the action. Not only that, but in the ultimate *in medias res* flex, we later find out that 1977's *Star Wars* is actually the fourth episode and drops us into the middle of a nine-part saga! Is your mind blown yet? This is exactly how you should create your short form video stories. Jump straight into it. You don't have time for the preamble.

In fact, in the era of short form video, you don't have time for any of these old conventions, though many marketers sometimes still cling to them. You are challenged now, more than ever, to get to the point of your message faster. There is too much demand, too little time, too many options, and too little attention to slowly ease your way into stories anymore. Okay, so if you cut the long list of credits in the beginning, what else can you lose that normally appears before the story starts? Much like the production company credits before a film (e.g. ABC Productions presents... a John Doe film), one pattern I've seen used is for companies to use their logos, or their clients' logos, in the beginning of the video. What for? What's compelling about that? Is your logo going to make the audience scoot to the edge of their seats, begging for what happens next? People don't care about your logo. In fact, no one wants to see your ad. They only care about themselves and their time and you're wasting it. Scrap the logo at the beginning! If you want to "tag" the video to reinforce your brand, do so at the end of the video or in a digital "watermark" in the lower corner of the frame. Don't waste people's time with it in the beginning, or else they will scroll past. Besides, it's not like people will find your video somewhere in the wilderness with no context as to what it is or where it's from. 99% of the time it will be posted from your (or your client's) channel, which would already have your name on it! Point is: it adds nothing to the viewer experience. And the viewer is who you need to care about.

What else? How about the title of your video, if you have one? These wouldn't be used as much in a short social media video, but in something that might be considered more of a documentary, it could be. Shouldn't a title appear at the beginning of the video? Not necessarily. When I was creating my 12-part docuseries for the Neuroendocrine Cancer Foundation, we started each video by fading up the episode title in white text. Then I noticed how many "3 second views" we had versus people who watched the whole six minute video. Three second views are what Facebook's analytics count as a video view (i.e. they must watch at least three seconds for it to count), but they also show you who watched what percentage of the video. There was a significant gap in our videos. When I rewatched them thinking about this, I noticed that we started with a black screen, slowly faded up our creative title (that had no relevance yet since we hadn't introduced our characters), slowly faded back to black, and *then* started our story. Sometimes that took like 20 seconds! People were gone long before the story even started. After episode three, we pivoted and made 30 second "hooks" in the beginning that pulled the audience into our character's story, and *then* brought up the title, once we already had them in. Our view count went up immediately.

Now, let's go even further. What about the classic fade in from black? This is a cornerstone of traditional filmmaking, as every screenwriter knows those first two words that start off every screenplay: "FADE IN." It's become the default. But there are a few issues that I've noticed recently that fading in can actually hinder your online presence and branding. On LinkedIn, which is a business social network and a prime place you might upload your business videos, their system doesn't allow you to choose a frame from the video to use as a cover image, or thumbnail. For those that don't know what a thumbnail is, it's a still image that serves as a preview for your video before your audience presses play. It's crucial because this image, along with the copy or caption, will be what first catches someone's attention and moves them to click the play button or scroll past. And a compelling image will jump out to them much faster than text they have to read, so the picture that serves as your thumbnail is a significant decision. On LinkedIn, unless you create and upload your own still image—which many people don't have the skills, time, or money to do—the platform will automatically select your first frame as the thumbnail. If you fade up from black, guess what? That means under your pithy caption that you worked for days to write, you have a black rectangle or square. And your audience is most likely gone. The other place I see this insidious black cover image is on Instagram. On Instagram, you actually can choose your thumbnail, or "cover image" as they call it, from a still frame of your video or uploaded on you've created from your phone's Camera Roll. But this step in the uploading process of a video is often overlooked by beginner Instagram users. It's not a big deal, as the video autoplays, but if you look at someone's profile full of beautiful images and then see a black square for one, it seems like a mistake at best and at worst, it doesn't compel them to watch the video. You need images that grab peoples' attention fast and no image at all just ain't cutting it.

All of these small details won't make a great story *bad*, per se. But they stand a great chance at making a great story go unwatched. And the point of telling a story is to impact your audience. There are so many habits that we assume because "that's the way it's always been done" or because they were considered "best practices" at one time. I urge you to think about what your story is trying to accomplish—what message it is trying to deliver to which audience—and find the most efficient way to get there. Your goal should be for each piece of your video to compel your audience to want to watch what happens next. It starts with an enticing and interesting cover image and a title or description that connects with the audience emotionally. Then each second of your video must be designed to keep them watching until the end. And the shorter your video is, the more chance you have of getting them to. Make sure to include all the essential elements of a good story (problem, journey, resolution) and make sure you include nothing more.

Chapter 8
HOW TO TELL A STORY IN SIX SECONDS

THE GOOD PROBLEM

French philosopher and mathematician, Blaise Pascal, once wrote, in his series *Lettres Provinciales*, "I have made this longer than usual because I have not had time to make it shorter."[19] But like all cool quotes, of course it eventually got attributed to Mark Twain.

In the current age of social media, you are tasked with the goal of getting your messages to the hearts and minds of your audience almost instantly. I've actually read articles about how marketers should have a "one second strategy" for their videos. After what we talked about in the previous chapter, I don't disagree with that. The ad length standards have dramatically decreased in recent years. So just like Pascal, Twain, and many others that have stated similar thoughts, that means your work has dramatically increased. What marketers used to be tasked with achieving in 60 seconds turned into 30 seconds. 30 turned into 15. 15 became 10 and 10 eventually went all the way down to six seconds. In 2016, YouTube came out with non-skippable six second ads they referred to as "bumper" ads and challenged the advertising world to tell a story in the shortest time block ever offered. Quickly, the ad world adjusted and adopted these little "bites" in new ways. Soon, six second ads became options on other social media platforms like Snapchat and Twitter. They went from social media to prime time broadcast television events like National Football League games and even baseball's World Series. With six second ads, networks broadcasting those events wouldn't even have to cut away to full commercial break to air a six second ad. That meant they could bring in additional revenue with this new ad type. Competitions popped up left and right to determine the best six second ads. Panels were held at conferences, articles were written, and the advertising world was set ablaze trying to figure out how to make the best ad possible in just six seconds.

But there was a problem that they all suffered from: no one could quite figure out how to emotionally connect with their audience in six seconds or less. Sure, they could make people laugh (like in the days of the now-defunct app, Vine), but could they make them cry? Sure, they could stimulate their senses with flashes and funky visuals, but could they move them emotionally to inspire real action? This was what made longer form ads so successful and stick in the minds and hearts of people for years to come, like the Budweiser "Lost Dog" Super Bowl ad that showed the Budweiser Clydesdales rescuing a lost dog from their farm. If you haven't seen it, it's a tearjerker. And it's one of the most memorable Super Bowl ads of all time.

So the question arose: can you actually tell an emotional story in six seconds? That is what I set out to do when I started my company.

Along that journey, I discovered good news and bad news. I always like to hear the bad news first so I end on a good note, so that's how you're going to hear it. Bad news: It is, in fact, incredibly hard to tell a story that evokes emotion in six seconds. Good news: To do it, however, only requires you to know how to do all the things you've learned already in this book. So you already have the tools to tell a six second story! You just have to do it at hyper-speed.

So in the interest of getting to the point fast, let's break it down.

ONE MESSAGE

We talked about cutting the fat in Chapter Seven and how to reduce the points you're trying to make in one video. You don't have time for multiple messages in a 15 second story, much less a six second one. Choose the one core message of your story and don't try to squeeze anything else into it. Is it about a product feature? Is it about a feeling or cause? Is it about your new service? You can always tell as many six second stories as your budget and resources allow. But for the message of your story, pick one and only one.

In 2019, my company was hired by a nonprofit called Student U to tell one of their Success Stories in a five minute documentary, as well as three six-second ads for social media ads. Student U is a community organization that helps first-generation college students succeed before, during, and after their college experience. In doing so, they help create a more equitable community by making new leaders and addressing the biggest cause of inequity: lack of education. One of their best Success Stories was a young woman named Nia. She grew up in a poor neighborhood with four younger brothers and found herself often having to take care of them while her mother worked multiple jobs to cover their bills. At a young age, Nia realized that she could easily become just a product of that environment and the only way out of that was to get an education. In came Student U. They helped her carve out her path to college and she got a full ride to the University of North Carolina (go Tar Heels!). Even though Nia thought she would become a doctor, she decided to help the youth like Student U had done for her and became a teacher at a school in Washington, D.C. that has a similar mission.

It was a perfect story for Student U to tell and I could easily see why they chose Nia. This is just one of their Success Stories but it demonstrates the snowball effect of their work, as Nia is now impacting so many other future community leaders, herself. When we told the five minute story, we showed all about what had inspired Nia, how she felt when she got her college acceptance letter (she screamed out loud on a public bus!) and what made her decide to make the switch from medical school to education—one that in many ways was a sacrifice on her part. But for the six second stories, we only had time to focus on one concept or theme. Our themes were "Fearless Leader," "Confidence," and "Own My Story." The first one is what Student U hoped to create out of Nia, the second is what they gave her to make her that fearless leader, and the third is what she was able to do once she became one. For each one of these themes, we told a micro story of where Nia was before Student U came into her life, what she wanted, and then how she was able to obtain that—positioning Student U and the "guide" or mentor that helped her get there. Remember how to do that from Chapter Four's outline of a Success Story?

When you have only six seconds to tell a story, you have to grab the audience's attention fast. A good image is an easy way to do that. The visuals in Nia's stories were key to "show, not tell," as well as grab the viewers' attention quickly. For "Fearless Leader" we started on a shot from a young smiling Nia. A picture of a child always works because: 1) people can relate to it since they usually reflect on childhood with nostalgia, and 2) people typically want all children to grow into healthy, successful adults, so they root for them automatically. Your audience is already hooked when they see a smiling kid. But then you juxtapose that by then showing a poised, confident woman, and BOOM, there you have it—a fearless leader. We used the same technique for the other two ads. For "Confidence" we relied on a static closeup of her big smile (which is honestly breathtaking) and the slightest zoom into her shining eyes. It screamed "confidence." Finally, for "Own My Story" we showed a 17-year-old Nia standing on stage confidently and announcing her decision to go to UNC. Our visuals were carefully selected to grab the audience's attention, as well as complement Nia's voiceover, which drove the story forward.

You don't have time for a lot of shots in a six second story, so you have to make them count. Finally, we ended on a simple logo and tag from Student U: "Empowering Students. Building Leaders. Changing Communities." This was a brand awareness campaign, as they were undergoing a brand revamp and wanted to expand their reach so they could impact more students. Because of that, the CTA (call to action) was for viewers to learn about their organization. The logo and quick tagline did that, and the website gave them a direction to take for more information. If this were a six second ad for your product, newsletter signup, special offer on a service, etc., the CTA would need to clearly communicate what you want them to do (e.g. "click here," "visit us at....," or "buy now while supplies last!"). Just like the theme and visuals, you have no time for confusion or competition with your CTA. Keep it to one simple, clear action you want them to take.

DON'T JUST CUT A LONGER STORY DOWN

One of the biggest mistakes that brands make—and even the big brands do this— is to take longer content that has been created already and just chop it down to a six or ten second version. This is a mistake. Like many creative decisions, the inspiration behind this idea is influenced by budget. Marketers and executives think: why create a new ad from scratch when you have an ad already created? There are even whole companies now that exist to do this for creators. Most people understand the challenge of taking a six second story and expanding it to 30 seconds (you have to create 24 more seconds of material!), but few understand the challenge of going from 30 seconds down to six ("Can't we just cut it down to the setup and punchline?"). Each story is its own narrative and must have its own arc. And the scenes and shots that make that arc are unique to each story. Sure, you can have a six second version of an ad as well as a 30 second version, but they both have to be scripted, shot, and edited to show the unique rise and fall of each one's arc. They cannot be abridged versions. It's been tried again and again and it just doesn't hit the audience in the same way.

In 2018, my company was hired by a custom remodeling company who took historic homes in their community and fully restored them while maintaining their character and certain architectural features that highlighted its original era. The company, CQC

Home, was scaling fast and becoming one of the top companies in their market. But they had a problem that was holding them back from their growth potential. They couldn't find quality workers that would help them grow while maintaining the integrity of their work (after all, the "Q" stood for "quality"). So they decided to use marketing videos to procure top talent in the area—a decision I am still impressed by for a local company with no one advising them. They hired us to create a two minute documentary for their "About Us" page on their website, one 30-second social media ad, one 15-second ad, and five six-second ads. They had some great stories to tell. One of the best was that of a young man named Dickon, who came to them as a day laborer making $12 an hour and within just a few years became their construction manager, earning over six figures. He had a great look, a British accent, and a hell of a story. The team at CQC Home knew this was one they had to share, so they asked us to do it twice—once in a 6-second ad and once in the 15-second version.

Dickon's voiceover for the six-second version went like this: "As soon as CQC hired me, things started to change. My work improved. As a result, this year I've had the opportunity to earn $100,000."

Okay, there is most of a story there. Or at least there is the result of a story. But a story, as you've learned, is all about the transformation that a character goes through—the struggle they experience and how they overcome it. We needed to establish what "things" specifically started to change in Dickon's story. We were missing that crucial element of establishing the character and the conflict they faced.

Now, compare that to Dickon's 1- second voiceover: "I started off in the industry earning $12 an hour scraping paint off of staircases. As soon as CQC hired me, things started to change. I grew as a person. My work improved. As a result, this year I've had the opportunity to earn $100,000. And that makes me feel pretty good."

See the differences? This story was exponentially better because of three additions. First, the audience now knew who Dickon is and where he came from—the bottom. That made his rise to construction manager and its accompanying salary even greater. Plus, they knew the struggle he went through. Have you ever scraped paint off of staircases all day? I did it one summer in high school. Trust me, it's a conflict you'd want to overcome. And then the audience knew that in order to get out of that struggle, CQC came along to help him (positioning themselves as "the guide" in this Success Story). Secondly—and though it was a small addition, it was important—that little line "I grew as a person." was such a great complement to the line "My work improved." Now the audience could clearly see that CQC did a complete job of mentoring him and it wasn't just his work that helped him rise to his new position. It was his growth as a person and leader. Furthermore, this reinforced CQC's narrative of creating a "family" dynamic among their team, where their goal is to help everyone achieve their dreams. And lastly, there was that final line. "And that makes me feel pretty good." You'll have to imagine the coy little smile that went along with it. You know how well faces convey real meaning. So CQC's audience already knew how Dickon was changed as a person ($12/hr to $100,000/yr and became a leader), but this little line lets us know that he's really happy about it. He's won. It's an exclamation mark on the story that also leaves the audience feeling good. If Dickon could feel that way working for CQC, perhaps so could their target audience (potential new hires).

And that was the message.

The 15-second version was the story. The six-second version was just a shortened version of that and it clearly suffered because of it. This happens all the time when brands shoot traditional 30-second ads for broadcast television and then create six-second versions for their social channels. They don't work the same way and brands wonder why. They don't work because there are essential parts missing—like the "before" in Dickon's story. The audience needed to see that change happen to really feel his story. As you learned in Chapter Seven, each story— like a joke—should only consist of the essential parts. And just as Bill Burr said, if you remove one word (or one essential part of the story, we can say), the story won't work. So if your 30-second video only consists of essential parts for that story, you would lose several of them by chopping it down to six seconds. And your story will suffer.

MASTER THE TWO MOMENTS OF CHANGE

When telling a six-second story, it still has to have an arc. It's a very small arc and you can't take a lot of time for the rising action to climb towards the climax. But you tell a six-second story essentially the same way you tell any story. You start with a normal world in balance, then a problem disrupts that balance, there's a quest to solve that problem, a resolution to that problem, and then the restoration of balance in a new way. Or simply like I've reminded you throughout the book: a problem, a journey, and a resolution. There are a myriad of different takes and approaches on story structure, but they all reflect the same fundamental journey. The better you understand the arc, the more you can understand how to craft a story that works in just six seconds. You already learned about basic story structure back in Chapter Three, but now we are going to dive a little bit deeper into some storytelling formulas, so you can more clearly recognize the bare bone essentials that they all have. Once you can do that, you will know what elements you need when telling a story in as few as six seconds.

22 STEPS TO BECOMING A MASTER STORYTELLER

John Truby, famed screenwriting teacher who has consulted on over 1000 scripts, has the "22 Steps to Becoming a Master Storyteller." Here are those 22 steps:

1. Self-Realization, Need, Desire
2. Ghost & Story World
3. Weakness and Need
4. Inciting Event
5. Desire
6. Ally or Allies
7. Opponent and/or Mystery
8. Fake-ally Opponent
9. First Revelation and Decision: Changed Desire and Motive
10. Plan
11. Opponent's Plan and Main Counter Attack
12. Drive
13. Attack by Ally
14. Apparent Defeat

15. Second Revelation and Decision: Obsessive Drive, Changed Desire and Motive
16. Audience Revelation
17. Third Revelation and Decision
18. Gate, Gauntlet, Visit to Death
19. Battle
20. Self-Revelation
21. Moral Decision
22. New Equilibrium

THE HERO'S JOURNEY

I've mentioned this classic story structure several times now, but haven't shown you the whole journey yet broken down. Joseph Campbell, in his now-legendary book *The Hero with a Thousand Faces* (partially made even more famous by George Lucas admitting it was the template for *Star Wars*) broke down his take on the monomyth, "The Hero's Journey," into 17 stages:

1. The Call to Adventure
2. Refusal of the Call
3. Supernatural Aid
4. The Crossing of the First Threshold
5. Belly of the Whale
6. Road of Trials
7. The Meeting with the Goddess
8. Woman as the Temptress
9. Atonement with the Father/Abyss
10. Apotheosis
11. The Ultimate Boon

12. Refusal of the Return
13. The Magic Flight
14. Rescue from Without
15. The Crossing of the Return Threshold
16. Master of the Two Worlds
17. Freedom to Live

THE STORY SPINE

Kenn Adams, long form improvisation instructor created and uses the eight steps of The Story Spine—as well as a little company called Pixar, which got the format from him. I already mentioned this one in detail back in Chapter Three. But because I love it so much, and it's so effective, it's worth repeating. Here it is again.

1. Once upon a time there was _____.
2. And every day _____.
3. But, one day _____.
4. And because of this, _____.
5. And because of this, _____.
6. And because of this, _____.
7. Until finally, _____.
8. And ever since that day, _____.

FREYTAG'S PYRAMID

Gustav Freytag, William Shakespeare, John Yorke, and many others have sworn by the symmetrical five act structure.

1. Exposition
2. Rising Action
3. Climax
4. Falling Action
5. Denouement

THE TWO MOMENTS OF CHANGE

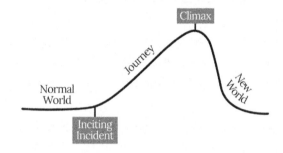

THE THREE-ACT STRUCTURE

And way back in 335 BCE, Plato's student Aristotle wrote Poetics—probably the first book on dramatic theory out of what has now got to be in the gazillions. In it, he described what each "whole story" must have:

1. A beginning
2. A middle
3. An end

"A beginning is that which is not itself necessarily after anything else, and which has naturally something else after it. An end is that which is naturally after something itself, either as its necessary or usual consequent, and with nothing else after it. And a middle, that which is by nature after one thing and has also another after it."

But no matter how many steps or stages different experts and theorists use for story structure templates, when you zoom all the way out and look at them, they all come back to the same basic shape of the arc. And the rise and fall of those arcs are driven by two specific and significant moments of change. The first one is the change that happens to the character (at the inciting incident) and sets them off on their quest to resolve the problem it creates. This is almost always from an external force. The second change happens *within* the character (at the climax) that allows them to find what they need to overcome the problem. It comes from an internal force. In order to get your audience to resonate with your character and the struggles of their journey, you must master understanding those two moments of change. Because they are all you will have time for.

If you were making a 90-minute feature film, you might have anywhere from 50-100 scenes to establishing the plot points surrounding those two pillars of the arc. But in a six-second ad, you won't have that luxury. You have to get to the point immediately. As I mentioned before, you can definitely tell a story with a beginning, middle, and end, in six seconds. But the goal of a great brand story is to evoke emotion in your audience and compel them to act. This is the challenge brands are facing when telling stories in such a super short format. Can you make them feel empathy? Love? Sadness? Hope? Those are the kinds of emotions that make stories memorable, that make people latch on to your message, and that compel them to follow your call to action. Mastering the two moments of change really comes down to understanding that your story is simply about cause and effect, before and after, problem and solution. Your character used to be in a certain situation with a problem and a goal, then something happened, and now they are somewhere else—in a better situation. Like the timeless lyrics of the hymn *Amazing Grace*, "I once was lost, but now I'm found."

In Nia's story for Student U, her voiceover for one six second story went like this: "Ever since I was a child, all I wanted was to be a fearless leader. And Student U made that possible." In those short six seconds, you can see where Nia once was and what she wanted, and then you can see that she was able to make the transformation to get there. In a six-second story, you don't have time for the lengthy Act II of a longer story, full of all the ups and downs and twists and turns that build up tension. You only have time for the problem and the resolution. But in that short amount of time, you must still find a way to create empathy with the character and evoke emotion in the audience. The best way to do that is to use unique details in Act One that the audience can relate to—the fact that she was a child as well as her desire to become a leader (more on this in a bit). Then, you have to close the loop and show that your character overcame her obstacle and achieved her goal, which elevates those levels of dopamine and oxytocin described back in Chapter Three. The key to her transformation, and the key to brand storytelling, is the positioning of Student U in the story as the agent of that transformation. The audience sees that the lessons learned to make the transformation came from her relationship with Student U. But, they don't see *how* it happened... and that's what leaves the audience wanting to learn more.

MAKE YOUR STORIES INTO A SERIES

When your audience is left in that state of wanting to see more, what do you do? You give it to them! Six-second stories are the perfect opportunity to string out smaller pieces of a larger narrative in a series or campaign. The days of creating one brand story video and plopping it on your website—and your tragically neglected YouTube so you can embed it on your website—are long gone. The need for consistent engaging content is here and it's been here for a while. I advise many of my clients to consider creating series because it is such a powerful way to grow a new audience and retain their current one. That, coupled with the fact that so many current platforms provide the perfect opportunity for short video series—Instagram Stories or Reels, YouTube, Tik Tok, Snapchat, and for sure some app that hasn't even become popular yet as of the publication of this book—create a demand for consistent content.

CLIFFHANGERS

Once upon a time, way back in the medieval age of the Middle East, there once was a king named Shahryār. Upon finding out about his wife cheating on him, he killed her and vowed to never trust another woman again. From that point on, he would only marry virgins and execute them the next morning after their wedding night, before they could have the chance to dishonor him. Until one day when the vizier's daughter Scheherazade offered herself up to be married to the king, against her father's wishes. On the night of the wedding, Scheherazade began to tell King Shahryār a story, but she didn't tell him the conclusion. Because of that, his cortisol levels and curiosity spiked in anticipation. And because of that, he postponed her execution so he could hear what happened. The next night, she concluded the first story but immediately started another, which she did not end, leaving the king hanging on to her thread yet again. She continued this process for 1001 nights until finally she told him that she had no more tales to tell. But over the course of all those nights, he had fallen in love with her and decided to spare her life. And the cliffhanger was born.

The cliffhanger went on to be a common device used in serial novels during the Victorian era with authors like Charles Dickens, "serials" in the early years of film where each week a theater would show the next installment, and more recently in serial television hits like *Breaking Bad* and *Game of Thrones*. Guess what? You can use the same tactic in your six-second stories. I doubt that your inability to craft great cliffhangers could result in your death like with King Shahryār and Scheherazade, but it certainly might result in losing your audience to the next shiny story that comes along— which, in its own way, is still an existential threat.

One way to do this is to have your six-second stories effectively serve as scenes of a larger story. When you are crafting a story—let's say a longer form story like a movie or a novel—the acts, sequences, and scenes within that story all fit together like a set of Russian matryoshka dolls. Each scene has its own arc which fits into the larger story arc. It has its own rising and falling action and its own conflict to be resolved before leading the audience to the next scene, sequence, or act. In this manner, you can use six second stories as scenes, leading your audience into the next six second story, while all part of a larger story arc. You can design them to immediately play in a sequence, like in a series of Instagram Stories, or you can have them as part of a larger ad campaign where you string them out over time. Either way, you must make sure of two things: 1) each six-second story in your ad should have its own complete arc, and 2) each six-second story should leave your audience with a question they want answered, driving them to watch the next story in your series. Remember when we talked about Nia's six-second story for Student U? Her voiceover read, "Ever since I was a child, all I wanted was to be a fearless leader. And Student U made that possible." We see that she made the change she needed to, and we see who helped her (Student U), but we don't see *how* Student U helped her. That leaves a great opportunity to fill that gap in the next six-second story if it were part of a series.

Any story should be a sequence of opening and closing loops that carry the audience through to the end. You open a loop and intrigue the audience, then you close it and satisfy their curiosity. You create a question and then you answer it. You raise the tension and then you release it. You establish a problem and then you resolve it. And so on. These are the ebbs and flows that make up the rhythm of storytelling. Cliffhangers are just open loops. But they're open loops that aren't closed until the next episode. If you use them correctly, they will keep your audience coming back and locked in to your stories. Then, at the end of your sequence, they will have fallen in love with you and your brand and make the decision to stay with you, instead of murder you like King Shahryār.

PARTS OF A WHOLE

There are other ways to create a series with your six second stories other than the cliffhanger model. Most products and services have multiple features that make them special—multiple solutions that they provide their customers. Great Cuts provides haircuts that are cheap, quick, and consistent with quality (even if the quality isn't that great). Apple creates tech products that are sleek in design, user-friendly, and super expensive (we'll just call that one "exclusive"). Whole Foods sells food that is healthy, sustainably produced, and also super expensive. We've already established that telling a six-second story is no time to be wordy and try to fit too much into your message. Another great strategy you can use for your campaign of stories is to have each story focus on one of the features your product or service provides your customers. Then, with a consistent theme and look, your next story pops up and continues the story of how you help your customers. When I created the series of six-second ads for CQC Home, the custom remodeling company, this is exactly what we did. Ray's story talked about the diversity of their employees. Latina's story showed how the company invested in her education. Shaun's story talked about how the company had a family feel. All of these qualities were representative of CQC Home's core values, but there's no way we could have covered them in a longer video. It would have been too confusing for the audience to understand what their takeaway was supposed to be. By breaking down the messaging CQC Home wanted to get across into a handful of six second stories, we were actually able to get more information across in less total running time. Not only that, but we had established a look and format that the audience understood and expected, so each video felt familiar even though it highlighted a different character and different value.

UNIFYING THEMES OR CHARACTERS

A third way you can effectively use six-second stories in a series is to play to those expectations of the audience by creating a unifying thread, character, or joke in all of your stories. One Saturday when I was a kid, I remember watching *Saved By the Bell* and still fantasizing about Kelly Kapowski when it cut to a commercial break. There was a commercial with some special mop airing that seemed a little phony, but I didn't pay it much mind because, ya know, Kelly was still on my mind. Just as it was nearing the end of the ad, the Energizer bunny came across the screen banging his bass drum and the characters in the mop ad turned in surprise to watch the bunny stroll across the screen. Then another commercial played—this one about a microwavable family meal—and the same thing happened! Ten seconds into what seemed like a food ad, the Energizer bunny came across the screen again! They did this three more times. It was a continuation of the initial Energizer ad and it was genius, playing into their slogan that it "keeps going... and going... and going." I have never forgotten it. After that initial campaign, the audience always knew what to expect with an Energizer ad and waited for it. So many brands have done similar things with recurring characters. The Geico gecko, the Aflac duck, Colonel Sanders of KFC, Flo from Progressive Insurance, the Budweiser Clydesdales, and so many more mascots and characters have filled this role. The audience comes to expect them on screen so much so that it feels inauthentic if they aren't featured in a commercial!

You don't just have to use characters for this method to be effective, either. Any unifying thread will work. Think about a joke or punchline that you might repeat. Have you ever heard a comedian that keeps calling back to the same joke throughout their set, even though the current joke started off differently than the initial one? Same concept. The point is, whether you use a joke, character, or some other thread, to set up an expectation in your audience's mind so that they are eagerly awaiting the reveal and you consistently deliver it right on time. And that's the same concept as opening and closing loops. That payoff fills them with dopamine and they associate that feeling with your brand! If they're looking at your product in a store aisle or deciding which company they should use for the service you provide, they will remember you for that. It's all about burying yourself in their minds and amplifying the recognition factor. Set up an expectation and deliver it. Nothing will feel more satisfying for them.

SMALL CHARACTER DETAILS THAT RESONATE QUICKLY

You remember from Chapter Three that a great character is the most crucial part of a great story. But to create a compelling character in six seconds is more than challenging. What normally takes a journey of ups and downs, setbacks and successes, and sacrifices and commitment to relate to your audience has to be achieved immediately. Since most of those ups and downs of the human experience happen in Act Two and you effectively lose your second act in a six-second story, you have to be creative on how you achieve resonance.

In Nia's Story for Student U, we referenced her past and where she came from. She said "I didn't want to be just a product of my environment." as the "before" part of her story and then we show that Student U helped her achieve the "after" of her succeeding in her goals. But the word "environment" is vague. It does give the audience a little bit to go on—they can make up their own version of exactly what she might've meant. But it doesn't give them much specific detail. The way we achieved that was simple. We showed a still image of a poor neighborhood with crime tape wrapped around an area. Nia alludes to criminal elements in her childhood during her longer story, but in the six-second story, there's no way we had the time to go there. In one picture, that lasted one second, we were able to communicate that information. With that addition, the audience knew that her "environment" was one where crime was normal. When she says she didn't want to be a product of that environment, the audience clearly knew what she meant was that she didn't want to get caught up in criminal activity or worse—become a statistic of someone who died because of their proximity to criminal activity.

Even though you don't have a lot of time to establish character, carefully chosen words can convey a lot of meaning. And even though a single word can't encapsulate all the complexities of one's character or their story, humans are meaning makers. Your audience's brains will fill in the gaps. But in order for your audience to fill those gaps with the right information, you have to be selective and specific with the wording you choose. Starting a story with "A mom went to the store with her kids." has some detail, but it doesn't evoke anything that the audience will resonate with deeply. A "mom" is certainly something they can latch onto, but there's not much more depth there. However, consider an alternative start to a story that reads like this: "A single mom braved the store with her twin toddlers." With just one extra word that probably wouldn't cost you a 1/16 of a second, you have conveyed so much more to the audience. You've given them specific details that will allow them to fill in that mom's story with their own information. If the audience has children, they understand what it's like to take a toddler to the story. It's exhausting. And it takes much more time than the trip to the store should take. But, to do so as a single parent, with *twins*?? Well that sounds like a suicide mission. Even if the audience has never been a single parent or doesn't have twins, they will understand what it probably means. They've at least had their kids alone for the weekend at some point. They probably cringe at the thought of having to do that every day. And they probably shiver with fear of thinking of two toddlers having simultaneous meltdowns in Aisle Six. Because of this, they will immediately empathize (and sympathize) with that character. With just a few carefully chosen words, they will now want her to succeed on her trip to the store. They will want to see her get that product that will help her manage her situation. And when it comes time for them to buy a product like that, they will remember the brand that helped that poor mommy bartering with crying two-year-olds by offering them any candy they wanted.

ALWAYS GIVE YOUR AUDIENCE A CALL TO ACTION

Finally, you must remember that six seconds is not a lot of time. That statement was written by my editor, Captain Obvious. But the point is, you have a lot that you need to include during those very short six seconds, so you have to be ruthless with your selection process. You cannot waste a millisecond. You need correct story structure, you need a compelling character, you need specific details that resonate, and you need to evoke emotion. But none of that matters, if you don't clearly communicate your call to action. The call to action should be right at the end and it should be very simple. "Shop now at blahblahblah.com." "Schedule your appointment today." "Ask us about our Spring Special." It should be written, not spoken. Our brains can process reading text much faster than hearing the words. Plus, it'll take three of your six seconds to say them. Your logo can pop up with the call to action to establish your brand recognition. But when you work as hard as you will crafting a great six second story, you cannot compromise that effort by limping across the finish line. You have to be clear. You have to make the sale (even if you aren't technically "selling" something, you're trying to convert your audience somehow). And to make the sale, you have to make the ask. When you get your target audience all drunk on that storytelling cocktail, you have to direct them to where you want to go. And if you've done your job well, they will follow.

Chapter 9
CONCLUSION

Now that you have read this book, you have all the skills you need to be a compelling storyteller, right? Well, kind of. In fact, you had them all along. Storytelling is part of being human. And you're human, aren't you? So the ability to tell stories is already inside of you. It's just my job to help you find it, and hopefully I have succeeded. Although, you may be thinking to yourself, "This all sounds great, Rain. I learned a lot, but I still don't know how I'm going to get the resources to pull this off on a grand scale," or "we just don't have the budget," or "how am I going to convince my boss/board to support this?" You might have the skills now and the know-how, but you're still concerned about acquiring the right tools for the job. Well to that I say, start with what you have.

If you have zero marketing budget and you don't even have any social media accounts, then whenever you are out and about, or at events, or at bake sale fundraisers, *use storytelling*. Talk to people about what you do and the problems that you solve. Tell them about unique characters that remind them of themselves or someone they love and how your business, product, or organization helped those people. Tell them about the moment you decided to change your life and dedicate yourself to your passion. Tell them stories! If all you have is a landing page of a website, use storytelling in your copy. Keep your messaging simple and to the point and lead them through your site step-by-step as if they are the hero of that journey. One door should unlock the next and lead them to the action you want them to take—to sign up for your newsletter, book a consulting call, or buy your new widget.

But the real advantage of being alive in the 21st Century is that almost all of us already have an extremely powerful tool in our pockets. If you own a smartphone, you don't need anything else to tell great brand stories. They have high resolution cameras and free editing tools so you can take professional-level photographs and use them on your social media sites like Instagram, Facebook, and Snapchat. Those same cameras shoot high definition and now 4k video that you can record at different frame rates, then edit on free mobile video editing applications and upload to your YouTube, Instagram, TikTok, or your own website. Those smartphones also have microphones—the same one you use to make phone calls—that can record your audio to release in a podcast. And there are voice recording apps that give you amazing tools to make those recordings even better. Smartphones have endless storytelling tools built inside them that you already have access to. You have no excuse. I know it's easy to make them, but trust me: some of the best content creators on the planet don't use top-notch equipment and tools. They use what they have access to and then build and grow accordingly, as their skills (and hopefully budgets) increase.

When I was shooting my documentary *Raise Up*, I faced a constant problem. The culture was so rooted in social media and sharing workouts via video, that everyone had a camera. In fact, some of these athletes had huge followings on YouTube and were even making a living off of creating highlight videos of their workouts and the competitions around the world. So as video became a bigger part of their lives and livelihoods, they invested more into it. That meant many of them had amazing equipment and some were even better than me at using it. That wasn't saying a lot, because as I have mentioned, I've never been a super technically skilled filmmaker, But the problem was that these people were "hobbyists" and I was the "professional" filmmaker, so they expected me to be very technically skilled. As I struggled with the limitations set upon me while making this film—like not having enough time, money, crew, or resources—I struggled to find out how I could tell this story unlike anyone else. But I kept thinking of how I needed those things if I was ever going to have the chance to be taken seriously as a filmmaker. And not having them made me feel like I was no better than any fan or spectator in the crowd shooting their own personal videos.

What happened was, I was forced to just lean into my situation and figure out a way to make it work. And by doing so, I had to embrace my limitations and find a way to make them work for me, instead of against me. After reading this book, you can probably tell I was born in the 1980s and raised as a "90s kid" based on my references. Well in the late 1980s/early 1990s the best boxer on the planet was "Iron" Mike Tyson. Mike Tyson became the youngest heavyweight champion of the world in history at the age of 20 and did so in the most electrifying manner the boxing world had ever seen—on many occasions, knocking out his opponents in mere seconds. But what many people don't know is that Mike never thought he'd be good enough to be one of history's great heavyweights. Actually, let me rephrase that. He thought he'd never be *tall* enough to be one of the greats. Standing at just 5 feet, 10 inches, Tyson thought that height was a necessary tool of boxing greatness (which makes sense when you think about the reach of a boxer, being able to strike an opponent from farther away is an advantage), especially since fighters like his hero, Muhammad Ali stood at six feet and three inches. But instead of listening to that voice in his head, and having a lot of help from his trainer Cus D'Amato, Tyson realized that it's not the tools he had that would make him great, but rather the skill he developed. And when he didn't have a tool he thought most great boxers did (height, in this case), he had to build his skill around that perceived weakness. Cus taught Mike how to easily slip past the taller opponent's jabs and get in close, where he could be dangerous. And instead of standing up as tall as possible, trying to replicate the taller boxer, and throwing straight punches, Cus taught Mike how to crouch down even lower, where the taller opponents couldn't reach him and to throw his jabs from vastly different angles. And because of that unique technique he developed, Tyson almost always caught his opponents with a punch they didn't see coming and eventually became one of the greatest of all times.

I did the same thing with my storytelling! Okay, bear with me a little bit while I compare myself to Mike Tyson. I'm not saying I'm one of the greatest storytellers of all time, but I am damn good. And I became that way because I stopped listening to that voice in my head telling me I had to have some certain tool in order to do so. I didn't have a lot of money, so I used the equipment that I could afford. I didn't have a team, so I learned how to use a lot of tools pretty well, instead of becoming great at just one of them.

And I wasn't gifted technically, so I kept my stories simple. And that technique worked for me because I put my main focus, time, and energy into understanding how human emotions worked and telling heartfelt human stories that targeted those emotions. Here's the cool thing. You can be like Mike Tyson, too! And in this version, I'll be your Cus D'Amato. What I want you to focus on is not that voice inside your head, trying to psych you out and tell you that you don't have the resources you need to create great video stories. I want you to focus on that voice in your heart, that is calling you to serve a specific group of people with your unique abilities. Like me and Mike Tyson, many times your resource restrictions will force you to make creative decisions that turn out better than if you had all the time and money you'd wish for. All you have to do is open up your heart to know what your story is really about. And then focus on delivering that message any way you can.

That being said, you now have more tools available to tell great stories than ever before in the history of humanity. You must learn to use them effectively, just as you have learned to tell compelling stories. You also have more access to those tools than you've ever had before. Those tools are also becoming more capable every day. There actually are movies shot on iPhones now—like the Duplass Brothers-produced film, *Tangerine*, that was shot on three iPhones in 2015. There are a myriad of mobile video editing apps that all allow users to edit video, still images, and audio, create stunning graphics and transitions, transcribe the audio into captions, and format the video for the platform you desire. There's "YouTube Video Builder," which creates short form video ads for you out of logos, still images, and graphics. There's Google's "Bumper Machine," which will automatically cut down your longer form videos and repurpose them into six-second bumper ads so you don't have to do any extra work. Pretty soon, automation is going to be the way of all technology. Artificial Intelligence will be able to replace a lot of the tasks that dominate our time and require so much of our minds to accomplish. But it won't replace our hearts.

AI is smart, meaning that it can learn new things, and perform its tasks with great speed, but it won't be able to be creative like a human will. It won't be able to tell a story. Actually, I should say that it *will* be able to tell a story, in terms of laying out the essential elements in a story structure. But it won't be able to conjure up the emotion in that story that makes a human connection. Back in the introduction of this book, you'll remember me referring to Yuval Noah Harari's book *Sapiens*, and how it shows that stories were what separated humans from the rest of the animal kingdom. Well, it is my firm belief that stories will still be what separates us in the future—but this time it will separate us from other forms of intelligence.

In Edward Hess and Katherine Ludwig's 2017 book, *Humility is the New Smart: Rethinking Human Excellence in the Smart Machine Age*, they discuss the skills humans will need to retain relevance in the age of automation. Hess says,

> "This book is the most important book I have written. We are on the leading-edge of a societal transformation that will be as challenging and transformative as the Industrial Revolution was for our ancestors and we as a society and as individuals are not ready for what is fixing to hit us. In the next 10-15 years, technology will take over millions of jobs including professional jobs. To stay relevant,

we human beings need to excel at doing those skills that technology won't be able to do well: higher order critical thinking, creativity, innovation and high emotional engagement with other humans.

We will be in a frantic footrace with the smart machines to stay relevant. Based on science and exemplars, we offer a new story about human excellence called NewSmart along with four NewSmart Behaviors that we believe will be necessary to excel at doing the skills that technology can't do well. Our book is a "how to" book – how to take your thinking, listening, relating and collaborating skills to much higher levels."[20]

Edward Hess calls those four skills "NewSmart Behaviors." I just call them storytelling skills. 1) Stories help you think about the different layers of a subject or issue—getting to the heart of the problem so you can find the best solution. 2) To be a great storyteller you must also be a great listener, letting your audience guide you so you can tell them the best stories that appeal to their struggles and needs. 3) The essence of storytelling is, and has always been, about relating to other humans. For people to care about a story, they must care about a character *in* the story. And to care about that character, they must relate to some part of them and their journey. Empathy. Empathy is everything in storytelling. Understanding what another person is going through and showing them a way forward with a story. 4) Finally, storytelling is a collaborative art. A "pas de deux" between the storyteller and the audience. It's a back-and-forth—an exchange of energy in the minds and in the hearts of people. The audience's brains fill up with oxytocin and they mirror the emotions of the characters. There is no story without the collaboration between the speaker and listener. The story transmitter and the story receiver. The storyteller and the storytellee. You get the point. To have a story, you must have them both.

The things that make you a storyteller are not tools like microphones, video cameras, computers, or mobile editing applications. They are human tools—like an open heart, empathy, compassion, kindness, creativity, connection, and community. These are things that machines can never replicate. And they are our way into the future, just like they have been since the beginning of humanity. Stop looking first for tools to help you tell your stories better. The tools will always change and they alone will not help you maximize the impact you have on your audience. Instead, look for the most efficient way to connect with them as humans. And that way, my compelling storyteller, is through their hearts. You can use new tools to accomplish your tasks faster, more easily, and for less money. Artificial intelligence can already create videos for you with tools like the Google Bumper Machine and YouTube Video Builder mentioned above. Other new tech tools can write your scripts, make flashy animation, add your titles and graphics, incorporate your call to action, post your videos, and even promote them. But they won't connect with the people you are speaking to. That takes human emotion. Like I said way back when I was making Raise Up: when it comes to storytelling, to making art, to creating connection, and inspiring people to be great, "it's the (hu)man, not the machine."

Guess what all this means? It means that you have all the tools you need to start telling compelling stories right now. Because if you're reading this, you're human (unless you're a robot). And to be human is to be a storyteller. So you're already, in fact, a great storyteller.

You just need to start telling your stories.

ENDNOTES

1. "Number of social network users in the United States from 2017 to 2026." *Statista*, Statista Research Department, 2021, www.statista.com/statistics/278409/number-of-social-network-users-in-the-united-states/#statisticContainer.

2. King, Stephen. *On Writing: A Memoir of the Craft*, Scribner, 2000.

3. Harari, Yuval Noah, *Sapiens: A Brief History of Humankind*, Harvill Secker, 2014.

4. Plutarch, *Life of Nicias*, XXIX.2-3.

5. Harari, *Sapiens*, 2014.

6. Godin, Seth. *This is Marketing: You Can't Be Seen Until You Learn to See*, Portfolio Penguin, 2018.

7. Godin, Seth. "Internet Marketing for Smart People Radio." Interview by Robert Bruce. *Copyblogger*, May 2012.

8. Stephens, Greg J., Silbert, Lauren J., & Hasson, Uri. "Speaker–listener neural coupling underlies successful communication." *Proceedings of the National Academy of Science*, 107 (32), August 10, 2010, 14425-14430, www.pnas.org/content/107/32/14425.short.

9. Zak, Dr. Paul J. "Why Your Brain Loves Good Storytelling." *Harvard Business Review*, October 28, 2014, www.hbr.org/2014/10/why-your-brain-loves-good-storytelling

10. Cassera, Melissa. "Multi-passion-itis with Melissa Cassera." Interview by Rain Bennett. *The Storytelling Lab*, May 16, 2019. www.rainbennett.com/post/multi-passion-itis-with-melissa-cassera

11. Simpson, William. "Myths & Monsters with William Simpson." Interview by Rain Bennett. *The Storytelling Lab*, April 18, 2019. www.rainbennett.com/post/myths-monsters-with-william-simpson

12. Leisure, Cora. "Cross-Modality Information Transfer: A Hypothesis about the Relationship among Prehistoric Cave Paintings, Symbolic

Thinking, and the Emergence of Language" *Frontiers in Psychology* (Toronto: University of Toronto Press, 2002), 100

13. McQuivey, Dr. James. "How Video Will Take Over the World." *Forrester.* June 17, 2008. www.forrester.com/report/How-video-Will-Take-Over-The-World/RES44199

14. Kizirian, Antranik. "The Eye and Vision." https://antranik.org/the-eye-and-vision/

15. Cisco Visual Networking Index: Forecast and Trends, 2017 - 2022. 2019. www.twiki.cern.ch/twiki/pub/HEPIX/TechwatchNetwork/HtwNetworkDocuments/white-paper-c11-741490.pdf

16. Perrin, Andrew. "One-in-five Americans now listen to audiobooks." *Pew Research Center,* September 25, 2019. www.pewresearch.org/fact-tank/2019/09/25/one-in-five-americans-now-listen-to-audiobooks/

17. Winn, Ross. "2021 Podcast Stats & Facts." *Podcast Insights,* August 25, 2021. www.podcastinsights.com/podcast-statistics/

18. Pinvidic, Brant. *The 3-Minute Rule.* Portfolio, 2019.

19. Pascal, Blaise. *Les Provinciales,* or, *The Mystery of Jesuitisme,* translated into English], Second Edition Corrected, Letter 16: Postscript, Printed for Richard Royston, London.

20. Hess, Edward D., Ludwig, Katherine. *Humility is the New Smart.* Dreamscape Media. 2017.

ACKNOWLEDGMENTS

I first started this book in January 2019, naively thinking I'd be done with the first draft by the end of Q1 and release the book later that year. Boy was I wrong.

And I can't even blame it on the global pandemic of 2020, which is quite convenient for blaming.

I blame it on two things: life and the eternal quest to learn.

The good news is that because it took longer than I initially anticipated, I became a better storyteller during that time and learned a lot more. Because of that, I believe the book is much more valuable to you.

But during the three years I've worked on this book, I had people stand by my side, help me along the way, and push me towards the finish line.

To those people, I owe a tremendous gratitude.

First, to my Six Second Stories (the business) team. That includes Dave Bennett and Khristen Wells, the two first people to join the team when it was in its infancy. They both brought a tremendous value and bore with me while I tried to figure out what direction to take.

The next year, I added Audrey Curelop and Anna Norwood, who helped our little company take the next leap and figure out the recipe for creating consistent content for clients on a large scale. They are both still good friends of mine and have moved on to creating their own projects and I'm so thrilled to see their work. Hell, Audrey's gonna be a lawyer! Hopefully they still think of me as a worthy mentor.

Chandler Comes took over Anna's roles of editing our in-house video projects in early 2020 and then took over Audrey's roles of producing *The Storytelling Lab* podcast and almost every other project we had in house after that. To do all that successfully, in the middle of a global pandemic that tried us all, is extremely impressive to me still. Furthermore, she edited this book. And that was basically a whole new job on its own, added to her ever-growing workload. Again, she handled it with grace and I couldn't have the book available to you without her.

But the person who has been with the Six Second Stories team for the longest (as well as the Flying Flounder team, and the B. Rain Bennett personal brand team), is Amy Scheidegger Ducos. Amy and I went to the same highschool, but didn't really know each other well back then. But she went to the same arts school that several of my friends attended at East Carolina University, so I kept an eye on her path from afar. Social media connected years later as social media does and when the opportunity arose for us to work together, she reached out and offered her services. For four years she's created movie posters for me, social media templates, proposals and onesheets, Powerpoint slides, all kinds of original graphics, and everything in between. But she did it—she does it—with a collaborative approach that makes the whole process feel like we are true partners. She listens to my hyper-particular requests, while also gently pushing back when her graphic design instincts tell her that we're heading in the wrong direction. And that approach always produces the best product. Most importantly, she designed this whole book. From the cover, to the images, to the placement of the words you are currently reading on this page. There is zero chance this book gets made without her.

Next, I owe my family more than the thanks I'm giving them right now. I owe them everything. I would not be the person I am today nor the one I strive to be tomorrow without them. My wife Maya has weighed in on countless book covers and title options, promoted me to her own communities, and even booked me a hotel to help me reach the finish line. A true partner. An entire support system right there in one person. Plus I love her a whole lot and she's funny.

Bellamy and Bishop, my children, well... I thanked them in the Dedication. It was kind of a backhanded compliment, because they were the two forces that inadvertently worked against me in this book writing process. But I'm still grateful for them. They give me a reason to write.

They give me a reason to live.

But I think the reason I ended up doing what I do for a living—specifically building a career off of telling stories and helping others tell theirs—has to be because of my original family. My mother, Geraldine McKinley, and my brother, Beau Bennett, are two of the most passionate and powerful storytellers I've ever known. Though I may have mastered the technical skills of storytelling a little bit better, they innately possessed the thing every great storyteller must have: the ability to elicit emotion from others. That is the foundation of human connection and they are both master connectors.

This book was written because I learned valuable lessons along my journey of being a filmmaker and video producer. Well, those lessons wouldn't exist without the clients whose work helped teach me those lessons. Many of them are used as case studies in this book. The biggest and best client I've had over the past decade has been the Neuroendocrine Cancer Foundation. Grace Goldstein has been the COO since I started working with them in 2011 and is the engine behind the foundation. Everything goes through her. I've learned so much about the nonprofit world by watching her work. Keith Warner, the CEO, has been the visionary behind each great leap the foundation has taken—always keeping them ahead of the technological curve. Along the way, he has become a great friend, mentor, and partner.

The writer, filmmaker, and storyteller that I've become is due in large part to the (award-winning!) work that the foundation and I have done together over the years. We've produced emotional documentaries and boring event videos, social media clips and live video shows—all with the missions of spreading awareness and educating people about this type of rare cancer. They gave me the chance to do great work in the film world and the medical world. And that has left me very fulfilled.

I must thank all of the clients mentioned in this book. They allowed me to tell their stories, but they also understood the power of storytelling in the first place. Ken and Ericka Combs created CQC Home and the "family" feel which that company upholds. I am grateful to have been let into that family for a brief time. Shae McCowen was the general manager who hired me and coordinated all my work with them. What a great company. I'm proud to have collaborated with them. Brandy Luce once saw me at a nonprofit storytelling workshop and we connected so well she brought Six Second Stories on to produce one of their biggest videos when they were rebranding the Student U organization. And finally, the American Red Cross of Eastern NC allowed me to tell a powerful story about a region that I care so much about. That wouldn't have been possible without Brittany Jennings and Barry Porter.

Many guests from my podcast, The Storytelling Lab, have found their way onto these pages. And many more have helped me become a better storyteller. But for their contributions to the book, I must wholeheartedly thank: Dr. Paul J. Zak, Melissa Cassera, Will Simpson, Kenn Adams, Brant Pinvidic, and Evan Carmichael.

Finally, over three years of writing and publishing this book, there have been MANY people who took the time to advise me and guide me along the process. Some of them ended up working with me to some extent professionally, but all of them influenced and informed the countless decisions one has to make when self-publishing their book. Emily Crookston is a phenomenal editor and her insight helped me understand the "big picture" of book writing. Lucinda Halpern convinced me to self-publish, even when it's her job to help authors get published! Ashley Bernardi taught me how (and when!) to best market a book, as well as the author. Dean Burrell taught me how to get a reader from one page to the next and keep the book in their hands. Annie Beth Brown has been a constant force of support and read a very early draft of the first three chapters. David Pisarra has coached me one-on-one and supported me from the sidelines since the idea to write this book popped in my (er... his) head. Angela Engel and her Collective Book Studio taught me everything there is to know about hybrid publishing—and their better-named "partner publishing." Lisa Ellison and Jill Rothenberg both weighed in on the book and the approach and audience I should focus on. Paul Kilpatrick called me out of the blue when he learned I was self-publishing just to share his knowledge from years of experience in the publishing industry. And Dr. Paul Zak, John Livesay, Mike Ganino, Melanie Deziel, Troy Sandidge, Annette Simmons, Alexa Carlin, and Kathy Klotz-Guest all read early copies and were gracious enough to say kind words about the book (and even let me print them!).

ABOUT THE AUTHOR

B. Rain Bennett is a two-time Emmy-nominated filmmaker, writer, keynote speaker, and storytelling coach with over 15 years of experience producing documentary films. He directed and produced his first feature length documentary by traveling the world with just a backpack and a Canon DSLR camera. That film, *Raise Up: The World is Our Gym* won "Best of the Fest" at the Hip Hop Film Festival and Bennett secured a deal with Red Bull Media House for worldwide release.

After over five years making this film with no financing, no crew, no big-name talent, and as a first-time director, he learned that no matter how under-resourced someone is when making a movie, if the story is great and targets the hearts of the audience, it can have a massive impact.

With his company Six Second Stories, Bennett helps small businesses, nonprofits, and entrepreneurs create short-form, heartfelt marketing videos to motivate their audiences to take action. He has been published in Huffington Post and Breaking Muscle and has written over 150 articles for his weekly column at Chapelboro.com. His films and articles have been seen around the world and he hosts a weekly podcast called The Storytelling Lab.

His mission is simple: to teach people how to leverage storytelling to grow their communities, deepen their connections, and maximize their impact in minimal time.

Bennett resides in Durham, North Carolina, where he is currently writing his first feature-length screenplay, as well as in post-production for his next feature documentary, *Finding Croatoan*, about the unending quest to solve the story of "America's oldest mystery," the Lost Colony of Roanoke Island.

In 2020, he released his second narrative short film, *The Casserole Brigade*, which won the Silver Award for "Best Short Dark Comedy" at the Independent Shorts Awards, "Best Comedy" at the Southern States Indie Fan Film Fest and the "Screenwriting Award of Merit" at the Foothills Film Festival.

www.rainbennett.com

Made in United States
Orlando, FL
09 January 2023

28424510R00115